Goal Setting
How To Revitalize Your Life

Setting And Achieving Your Goals The Smart Way

Raymond Le Blanc

Table Of Contents

Copyright & Dedication

This book is not completely comprehensive. Some readers may wish to consult additional books for advice.

Author: Raymond Le Blanc

Edition 1.1

Several paragraphs of this e-book have been first published in paperback format in Achieving Objectives Made Easy! ISBN9789079397037

Dedication
For Karin, Brigitte & Vincent, for all time.

Author Online
http://raymond-le-blanc.com

About The Book

Discover powerful goal setting techniques to turn around every area of your life—at home or at work.

Engaging and down-to-earth, author Le Blanc walks you step by step through practical goal setting techniques to enable you to reach previously unreachable dreams and goals.

You will quickly learn how to use this books information for your own success.

With Goal Setting you will

- Develop a mission and a vision for your career and personal life
- Learn strategies for setting and achieving goals
- Implement habits as a key to success
- Watch your dreams become reality
- Believe you can succeed and you will
- Achieve more
- Increase your pride and satisfaction
- Set goals and stick with them
- Increase your motivation to achieve
- Make your values and beliefs your allies
- Learn how to think positively
- Stay motivated, focused and balanced
- Cure yourself of the fear of failure
- Turn defeat into victory
- Use goals to help you grow
- Improve your self-confidence
- Drive yourself forward with focus
- Be the best you can be
- Revitalize your life

Sidebars

A sidebar is a side note that relates to the main discussion, but which breaks the flow of the main thought. It appears like this...

-----Sidebar-----
A sidebar is a side note that relates to the main discussion, but which breaks the
flow of the main thought. So I "tuck it away" to help the flow. It appears like this...

Preface

After finishing university as an economist and accepting my first post, I married, made a career and raised children.

Always too many things to do and too little time to do them all.

Having been diagnosed with and treated for a severe Panic Disorder, I decided to take my career down a new path.

After receiving a master's degree in psychology I made the transition from a banker to clinical psychologist and author.
I studied time management, goal setting, and self-management and enthusiastically applied this knowledge to other areas of my life.
I soon found I had more time for myself and my family.

The approach in this book blends existing ideas with my experience.
The valuable techniques I use in this approach are provided in this book.
They are the foremost (and easiest!) methods to enable you to make more time for yourself and to achieve your desired goals.
You will certainly become better equipped to Live The Life That You Really Want!

Introduction

We heap our daily schedules full of activities. Despite time-saving conveniences like cell phones, computers and the Internet, we rarely have enough time for our work, our families, friends, or ourselves. So many activities daily demand our attention that it can be difficult to make plans, even if those plans would ease our burdens down the road.

We are busy, but are we productive with our time or happy with the way we spend it?

Many people fail to achieve what they want and what they dream of simply because they haven't yet discovered the secrets of goal setting and time management.

Managing your time and setting goals are interwoven topics. A healthy time-management plan encompasses goal setting. Achieving goals is only possible when the time factor is considered. With the aid of this book, you will gain a necessary insight into goal setting and learn how to accomplish more than you thought possible.

Whether you are a newbie to goal setting or you've delved into similar books on the subject before, this book has a lot to offer you. It goes beyond presenting techniques; it teaches you, step by step, page by page, how to achieve what you've only dared to dream of before. That dream is now in reach.

It's time to go get it.

Throughout this book, you will be asked to answer questions that will help you on your way. It would be handy to grab a notebook or a journal (we'll call it a journal, for simplicity's sake) and a pen or pencil (or an electronic equivalent), and keep them within arm's reach.

To make the most effective use of this book, I recommend you read and put into practice just one simple step—only twenty minutes or so—a day, to start relieving your stress, reaching for success, and maybe even learn something surprising about yourself.

It's all in here. Enjoy creating the high-quality life you desire.

Let the journey begin.

Raymond Le Blanc

Tip 1: Use A Journal

Goal setting is one of the behaviors that separates successful people from unsuccessful people. If you're not satisfied with where you are in life right now, it's time for you to set some goals and start changing your life. Using a notebook like those made by Moleskine (or an equivalent) can help you to clarify your goals and achieve what you need to achieve.

Buying a *Moleskine*(1) notebook is a great way to kick off a goal setting session. Moleskine notebooks are ideal for goal setting because they are well made and many of them are very portable. You want to always be able to carry around your written goals with you, and a Moleskine notebook makes this possible.

- Using your notebook as a journal can help you solve problems. Write down a problem and your related feelings and emotions, and then brainstorm for possible solutions. This cannot only relieve stress, but also help you attain goals by providing an opportunity to work through problems, find solutions, and keep from getting 'stuck' in unhealthy patterns.
- Journaling fuels the imagination spirit and soon your ability to communicate on paper will help you to improve your interaction with others as well.
- Journaling is a great way to be creative. A blank page is a safe place to experiment with ideas that on the surface would seem far outside the realm of possibility. You benefit from the self-expression and increased awareness of your thoughts and feelings.
- You can write about all the things for which you are grateful each day. This form of journaling can help you feel more gratitude in your life as you develop the habit of noticing all the good in your life. This can decrease the stress that you feel, as well as help you realize all that you have available to you already.
- Journaling bears witness and provides the clues to how you think, learn, create and use intuition.

- Journaling focuses and refines your desires, needs as well as helping you at good decision-making and quality living.
- Using a journal allows you to unleash your goal and dream to paper, which provides the opportunity to visualize the outcomes in advance of taking action.

Your Moleskine and goal setting are not enough to achieve success. You need to take action every day to strive and achieve at least one of your goals. Give yourself a certain amount of time each day to focus on achieving a specific goal. Mark your progress in your Moleskine and allow yourself to feel proud of yourself when you succeed in accomplishing one of your goals.

(1) The author is not affiliated with Moleskine.

Tip 2: Consider Mind Mapping

For many people learning how to use a mind map for brainstorming and goal setting will be an exciting expansion of their current knowledge and skill set. In addition it can also be a better and easier way for you to take notes and study many other subjects as well.

For others it may first appear to be a bit of a challenge, but the good news is that once you learn more about them you will see just how easy and natural they can be to work with.

What Is A Mind Map

Basically a mind map is simply a visual diagram consisting primarily of :
- pictures or images which should be used to represent your key topics, ideas or tasks.
- keywords or keyword phrases that also capture the essences of a topic, idea or task.
- circles and line which can be one or multiple colors. These contain the images and show the connection or flow between topics, tasks or ideas.

When properly constructed a mind map can be used as a very effective whole-brain learning tool for generating, capturing and organizing ideas and information.

Images are associated with right brain holistic functions and keywords are associated with your left-brain analytical functions.

You should also you different color pens or markers, which help to stimulate your creativity and imagination which are right-brain functions.

Mind maps are more of a free form way of creating a to-do list or capturing ideas without having the constraint of needing to have everything listed in a sequential order.

This allows you to focus more of your attention on the task of capturing useful and relevant ideas as apposed to worrying about what order everything needs to be in.

Prioritizing and organizing the task is done in a separate step from capturing all the ideas and needed information.

How To Use A Mind map for brainstorming and goal setting

The good thing about doing brainstorming and goal setting to gather is that you are combining one creative activity with another, which works out really well. Here is a simple four step process that you can follow :

Step 1.) Start with your goal - Write it in the middle of a sheet of paper if possible create a picture or symbol to represent it and then circle it. On the outside of the circle you should write a keyword that accurately represents your topic.

Step 2.) Write down (in a free style form) other thoughts or ideas that come to mind that will be needed or supportive in achieving your goal. Circle them and draw a connection between them and your goal

Step 3.) You now need to add any sub task that may be needed to be completed for any task that will require a preceding action. For example, if you are creating a mind map for starting a business, your goal may be to become financially independent.

Prior to achieving that goal there will be quite a few major and minor milestones to reach along the way. After you have written down the major ones (like get your equipment and have your product created) you would then list the smaller tasks (like find the best vendor or get the best pricing, etc)

Step 4.) Once you have all of the items needed, you can subsequently organize them and make sure that everything is in a logical order.

In many cases you will find that working through this process will not only help your organize your thoughts and see the big picture, but it will also help to embed your goal and plans into your subconscious mind where they can take on a power of their own.

Recommended tools to use for mind mapping include :

+ A White board
+ A Notepad or sheet of paper
+ Software programs or Mind Mapping Apps

Example MindMap, by Nicoguaro,
http://en.wikipedia.org/wiki/File:MindMapGuidlines.svg

PART ONE: Introspection

1. Go Ahead - Dream

This book is about far more than how to set goals and manage your time. It's about how to use proven goal-setting techniques to help you succeed and to achieve what you've only dared to dream of. So let's cut right to it. What do you want? What will bring you happiness? What get's you excited? What are you passionate about?

Before you have concrete goals to write down in your journal, you need to start brainstorming. Brainstorming is a valuable process that a lot of prospective high achievers overlook. In order to best figure out what goals will help you accomplish what you really want in life, you need to get your creative juices flowing.

Start by jotting down all the different ideas you have about what you would like to accomplish in life. Use the first couple pages of your journal to write down everything that comes to mind. Don't leave anything out -- even if it seems ridiculous or improbable. You can always edit what you have written down later.

Next, you need to take the time to sift through your written ideas and pick out the goals you truly want. Go back over your written brainstormed ideas and circle the ones that appeal to you the most. After you have decided what you want to achieve, think about how you are going to go about achieving what you want to achicvc.

Set Goals that are Motivating

If what you want to accomplish is going to require that you do many different things, come up with a series of small goals that will help you to get where you want to go. Don't give yourself one immense complicated goal. Small, easily-accomplished goals are much easier to work on than huge, complex ones.

Write all your goals in your journal. Put a bookmark in the section of your journal where you have written down your goals. Everyday, make sure that you take the time to read your goals in the morning and the evening. You can also read your goals more often if you would like too. The more frequently you read your personal goals, the less likely it is that you will allow yourself to forget about them.

- Visiting Brazil
- Writing a novel
- Having a baby
- Designing and building a hang glider
- Attending a seminar on Non Violent Communication
- Getting a degree in psychology
- Learning a second language
- Living abroad for a year
- Starting an Internet business
- Finally losing that excessive weight
- Cycling from Amsterdam to Rome
- Buy my own beach house
- Earn an extra $200 monthly by December
- Get rid of the clutter on my attic

Remember the time when you were young. Free of mental baggage. Capable of doing and being anything you want. When your dreams involved being an astronaut, super woman, movie star or Florence Nightingale? The time when your fantasies where limitless and your possibilities seemed endless.
Before you started giving up on your dreams due to worry, fear, limiting beliefs and self-fulfilling prophesies planted into your mind by often well meaning adults?

Because of these feelings and fears, few of us attempt such grandiose dreams. Instead, we settle for the ordinary and as a result fall into a "reality" trap.
Vow to stop putting down your dreams!

What do you truly want? If you could do anything you wanted, how would you spend your time? What if you could start over with a clean slate? Where would you live? What will give you the thrill of a lifetime? Take a few minutes. Who would your friends be? Think about it.

This is the first—and a key—step toward achieving your goals. Let those long-awaited wants bubble to the surface. Keep in mind that this kind of dreaming is best done when you are feeling inspired and energized. Boundless. Because the quality of the goals you set for yourself makes all the difference between living a fulfilling life and just living an average life.

So go ahead dream and list it all. Write down whichever of your 'dreams' you consider important enough to want to achieve. If you find this difficult this list of goal categories may come in handy.
- Career Goals
- Education & Training Goals
- Family & Relationship Goals
- Health & Fitness Goals
- Home Improvement & Real Estate Goals
- Personal Finance Goals
- Personal Growth & Interest Goals
- Recreation & Leisure Goals
- Time Management & Organization Goals

Note:
This list of dreams/goals does not have to be accomplished in a year's time. Some might even never be accomplished. For instance, because at a later point they lose their appeal because they are just not that essential for you to pursue. And keep in mind that the best way to reach your goals is to focus on one paramount goal at a time. Focus, accomplish it, gain confidence and happiness and move on to the next goal.

Tip:
Goals must be in writing. An unwritten want is just a wish. If it's in writing, it's real, big, and the beginnings of a commitment.
Writing down your goal also makes the goal more powerful. It has been proven that when people write things down, they are more likely to focus on them and achieve their goals.

—————(Sidebar)—————

Often people focus on what they want to achieve in terms of having (I want a bigger house, a larger income, a faster car) or doing (I want to travel more, do more work outs, relax more) when goals are concerned. You may however want to consider putting "being" in the equation too (I want to be happy, fulfilled, that type of person or anything else you want to be).

Example: Goals/Dreams

Career Goals
> Writing a novel
> Starting an internet business

Educational & Training Goals
> Getting a degree in psychology

Family & Relationship Goals
> Having a baby

Health & Fitness Goals
> Losing that excessive weight

Home improvement & Real Estate Goals
> Buy my own beach house

Personal Finance Goals
> Earn an extra $200 monthly by December

Personal Growth & Interest Goals
> Attending a seminar on Non Violent Communication
> Learning a second language
> Living abroad for a year

Recreation & Leisure Goals
> Visiting Brazil
> Designing and building a hang glider
> Cycling from Amsterdam to Rome

Time Management & Organizational Goals
> Get rid of the clutter on the attic

2. Bucketlist

In the previous chapter, you were invited to jot down your dreams. In this chapter I'll invite you to add some more goals to your list. You may be familiar with the 2007 movie The Bucket List (starring Morgan Freeman & Jack Nicholson) in which two incurably ill men escape from a cancer ward and head off on a road trip with a wish list of things they want to do before they die.

Why should you want to create your own bucket list?
Mainly to motivate you to get out of your "lazy" chair and go for your dreams.
Odds are that you'll spend most of your time caught up in a myriad of day-to-day activities. If you don't live your life guided by personal goals and plans, that is what usually happens.
So a bucket list is like a master list of goals for your life.

To make your own bucket list it might come in handy to think what you would like to achieve, what you would like to experience and what activities you'd like to take part in and skills you'd like to develop.

You can find these in fields like:
- Career
- Charity & Community
- Creativity
- Education
- Family Life
- Health & Wellness
- House & Home
- Love & Relationships
- Personal Finance & Wealth
- Sports & Adventure
- Travel
- Etcetera

I added some examples to get you inspired.

(PS: Don't overdo it. Start by adding a maximum of 10 to your list)

- Learn Spanish
- Climb a volcano
- Go wild water rafting
- Lose 10 kg
- Buy a house
- Start exercising regularly
- Run my first marathon
- Go vegetarian for a month
- Obtain my nursing license
- Perfect my chili recipe
- Take my mom to the best US antique mall
- Write a novel
- Pay off all my debt
- Climb to the top of a volcano
- Travel Canada
- Meet my sponsored child
- Start a company
- Donate blood
- Declutter my home
- Learn to play oboe
- Fill a journal with inspiring quotes, lyrics & images
- Skinny dip in Iceland
- Get drivers license
- Visit New Zealand
- Donate bone marrow / stem cells
- Learn to belly dance
- Meditate at least three times/week
- Buy someone's holiday groceries
- Clean my room
- Visit iconic locations of WW II
- Find a new job
- Go parasailing
- Don't complain about anything for a week
- Make a bookshelf
- See the Northern Lights

- Own a plantation to offset my carbon footprint

—————(Sidebar)—————

There are various websites that might help you along in creating your own 'bucket list'. I didn't list them in any particular order. You are invited to find out if one suits your needs best.
Bucketlist 10,000 things to do before you die.
http://www.bucketlist.org

Day Zero is a place to record your goals, discover new challenges, and gain motivation to do them.
http://www.dayzeroproject.com
(Special attention http://www.dayzeroproject.com/feature/ for some inspiration)

My Life List®, the premiere social network for goal achievers. The tools you find here will help you create your Life List, act on your goals, and celebrate your accomplishments.
http://www.mylifelist.org

43 Things What do you want to do with your life?
http://www.43things.com

MySomeday. Dream Plan & Achieve.
http://www.mysomeday.com

Reaperlist. What will you do before The Reaper Comes?
http://reaperlist.com

Create your bucket list of ambitions, experiences and goals that matter to you, and see how many you can make happen just by having a list!
http://www.popclogs.com

SuperViva – Make a Life List and Find Things To Do for Your Bucket List
http://superviva.com

Example: Bucketlist

- Build a custom motorcycle
- Go to an IKEA in Sweden
- Try haggis in Scotland
- Write an iPhone application
- See the Hell Hole in Karakum Desert
- Trek the Inca Trail
- Visit the Titanic in a submarine
- Complete the NAUI rescue divers course
- Build an eco friendly home
- Learn to meditate

3. Your Current State of Affairs

By three methods we may learn wisdom: First, by reflection, which is noblest; Second, by imitation, which is easiest; and third by experience, which is the bitterest. ~ Confucius

You have 'dreamed' of what you want and written down a few solid goals. Excellent.

Now here's a question. Once you achieve those goals, will you enjoy happiness in all areas of your life?

Probably not all areas.
Living a balanced life is important because then we can be more content, more alive, and enjoy each day better. Living a balanced life means keeping balance in physical and spiritual aspects. So let's look at your current state of affairs to determine which other goals you may wish to consider to bring that balance and happiness. Let's gain clarity of your life right now.

Here is a excellent way to help you measure your success (happiness) in several fields:

Read the paragraphs below. Rate yourself on a scale of 1 to 100 (1 is low, 100 is high), asking yourself how satisfied you are with your finances and career, family and home, community and charity (your social side), spirituality and ethics, physical well-being and health, and mental and educational levels. Consider your answers carefully.

Finances and Career.
Feeling happy with your career or business is an important ingredient to obtaining happiness in other aspects of your life. Possessing a secure financial situation offers a reserve essential to feeling happy about yourself.
Are you financially secure? Are you happy with your career, job, or business, or are you suffering in this area? Have you achieved a satisfactory standard of living? How much is your income/monthly cash flow? How much do you save from there? Do you have any passive income streams? How much are your current assets? Have

you created a stable financial situation where your personal assets grow monthly? Have you planned for your children's education? What about your own retirement? Are you achieving your best?

My score _____

Family and Home.
Friends and family give us a sense of belonging and enable us to cope with the challenges of the world.
The love of one's spouse is a precious gift that continually needs to be worked on to grow. Raising a family can be a rich and rewarding experience and challenge. Establishing and preserving strong, productive family relations nurtures our self-esteem.

Do you have close, loving, family relationships? Have you realized your dream when it comes to your household and loved ones. Do you have a romantic partner? Do you spend quality time with your friends?
Be sure to use your own personal standards rather than society's standards. Have you forgiven anyone who has hurt you, and have they forgiven you? Do you talk with your family freely and openly? Do you thank each other for the things that you do well, or do you sabotage each other?

My score _____

Community and Charity.
We all are a part of a community. Having strong, flourishing relationships and skills to get along well with others is crucial in order to experience strong self-esteem. We crave to belong, we need to belong.

Do you make contacts easily, and do they help build your self-esteem, or are they people who drain your self-esteem? Is there at least one other person with whom you have a deep connections with ? Do you have many rewarding, close, and loving relationships? Do you have interests outside your career and family (for example, sports, theater, outdoor events)? Are you happy with your contributions to charities and to the community you belong to? Do you have a good social circle? Friends to hang out with, talk to, confide in, have fun with? Are you meeting new people? Have you found your life partner/soul mate? Is this a fulfilling relationship? Are you giving back to the society and the world?

My score_____

Spiritual Health.
The spiritual dimension is your center, your commitment to your value system. Good spiritual health inspires and uplifts you.

Do you take time regularly to read uplifting books or listen to personal development audios? Do you have your own clearly defined, written vision for what your life will be like, or do you merely go along with someone else's vision for your life? Are you in touch with your values, with your abilities, and with your life purpose? Are you living up to those personal values? Is religion important to you? If so, are you happy with the way you are practicing your religion?

My score _____

Physical Health.
Positive, vibrant confidence comes from taking the best possible care of our health. Physical health involves caring for your body—choosing the best foods, getting enough sleep, and exercising regularly. If we don't have a regular exercise program, eventually we will develop health problems. A good program builds your body's flexibility, strength and endurance. A new program should be started gradually, in harmony with the latest research findings.

How satisfied are you with your current level of physical health? Do you exercise regularly? Is your life style healthy? Do you have enough sleep/rest? Are you exercising regularly? Are you fit enough to do everything you want to do? Is your diet leading to ideal health, or do you regularly eat junk food?

My score _____
Mental Health.

It's vital that you keep your mind sharp by studying, writing, organizing as well as planning. Read frequently and open yourself to great hearts and minds.

Did you carry out the educational goals you set for yourself following high school graduation? Are you still growing and learning? Do you regularly invest in your continuing education? Do you take the time to do the hobbies and activities that you love to do? Are you achieving your highest potential? Are you being the best you can be?

My score _____

Emotional Health.
Emotional well-being involves how we think, feel and behave. Nobody feels full of joy, thinks positive thoughts and displays prudence all the time, but if you're in a good mood, it's much easier to enjoy life.

Are you content with the way you treat, respond to, and interact with others? When you're alone, are you content with the way you think of others and of yourself?

My score _____

Individuality.
Individuals tend to change their world in order to reach a desired state. Individuality is about being able to enjoy freely your own interests and point of view.

Are you happy with your individual space? Do you feel there is room beyond your personal space for your individuality? Do you feel liberated? Do you feel free to choose the outlook or lifestyle you desire? Do you feel you are free to stand by your own convictions? Do you respect and appreciate yourself? Do you love yourself? Do you value what you do?

My score _____

Next, record your answers on the following circular chart by putting a dot on the spoke of each respective category.

Assign the innermost notch on the wheel a value of 0, and the outer ring a value of 100. After you have marked all the spokes, connect your dots, creating your own wheel.

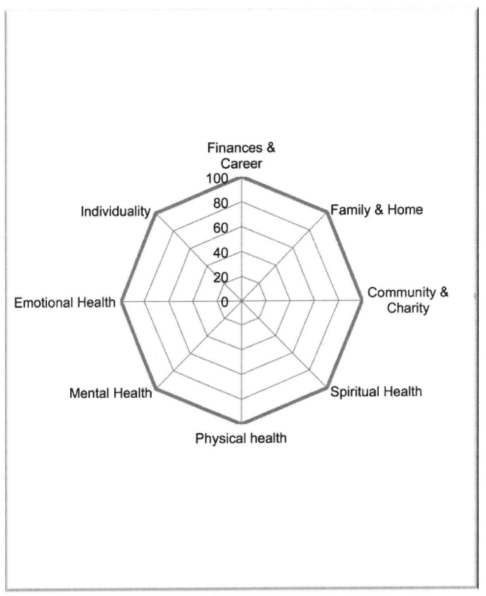

Figure: Blank current state of affairs

For example, it may look something like the example figure below:

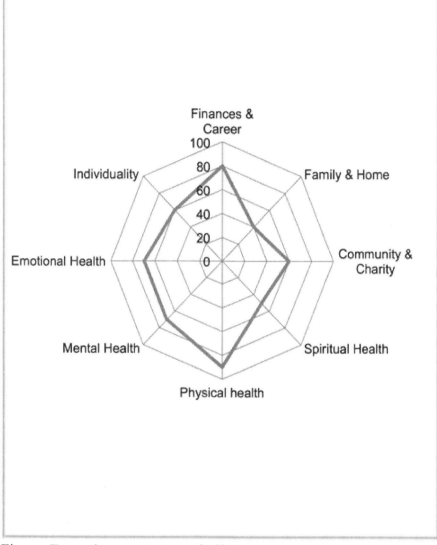

Figure: Example current state of affairs

This figure shows you a visual representation of a current state of affairs.
You can color the inside of the area marked by the thick line with a solid color if you prefer.

(These figures are inspired by the Wheel of life (Bhavacakra), an instructional figure in Buddhism.)

Now it's your turn.

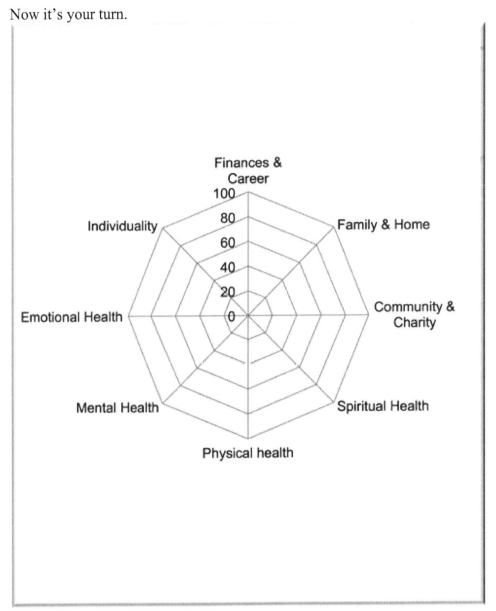

Figure: Your current state of affairs

The outcome of your current state of affairs shows your level of satisfaction with various aspects of your life. The more solid color there is, the more balance you have, and the happier you are. If your circle is lopsided, the low scores reveal areas on which you might want to focus your goal-setting efforts. If your wheel is round but small, you may want to set goals in all areas to expand your wheel and therefore your overall happiness.

Where might you benefit from making changes? Consider your low spots, the areas you are least satisfied with.

To the goals you already formulated for yourself, add the areas you want to improve upon (I want to improve upon:)

Combining the items from chapter 1 & 2 with the areas of life you want to improve on will give you a lot of food for thought.

Congratulations! You now have the beginnings of a few or several goals you would like to achieve.

The wheel can serve as a focal point from which you measure your change. I recommend you take a look at your state of affairs regularly. You can use the information your wheel provides to see in which areas you are showing improvement and where you may want to put in some extra work.

Note:
The "wheel" we used in our example is just one of the many ways to illustrate our point. You do not necessarily have to work with the 8 corners used in this example.
For instance you could use others like:

Work/Career
Is your work life fulfilling and nourishing? Do you enjoy your work? Are you currently on a excellent career path? Have you got just as much energy at the end of the day as you would at the start

Money

Are you free from financial stress of any kind? Are you completely satisfied with your current level of income? Do you feel you are on the right track?

Health

How do you feel - physically? Do you think you're fit? Are you receiving helpful care for whatever health challenges you experience?
Are you exercising regularly and eating for sustenance/pleasure and not emotional comfort?

Friends & Family

How do you rate your own relationship with your friends and family? Do you have a group of friends that stimulate you? Do you like being with your loved ones and do they support you?).

Relationships

Relationships are defined as your partner or loved one. Of course, if you are happy being single, then your relationship is measured in that regard. Are you pleased and excited with your relationships? Are you loved by those who mean the most to you?

Personal Growth

Are you living your life, not the life someone else designed for you or expected of you? Do you feel fully alive and full of energy? Are you evolving, not just improving, because you continually experiment? Have you done or are you doing any courses/coaching to improve yourself?

Fun & Recreation

Do you spend your leisure time totally enjoying your interests? Is your time off a joy to you? Are you having fun? You do take time off - don't you? Are you engaged in leisure activities outside of work? Do you have a plan to go to a place you have always wanted to go?

Physical Environment

Are you 100% satisfied with your physical surroundings? Do you live where you want? If in your control, is your work environment what you want?

—————(Sidebar)—————

This representation, using the form of a wheel (divided into 8 segments) gives you a snapshot of how you're doing. It is essentially a circle divided into segments that represent your different areas of life. You can use any number of segments you like. For instance not all segments have to play an important role in your life, right now. Choose the various aspects of your life that are important to you now. You could even focus on less than 8 areas. For instance only 3 or 4 you think are most important to you at any given time.
For Instance

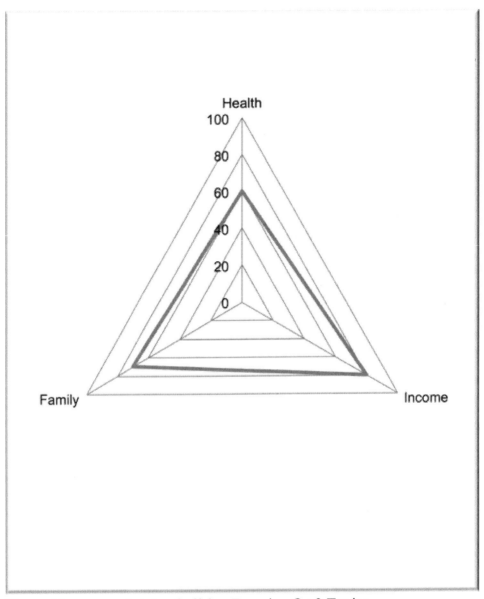

Figure: Your current state of affairs, Focusing On 3 Topics

4. Your Mission

You now have a list of goals you want to achieve for your personal, and perhaps professional, success and happiness.

So how do you make those plans happen?

It all begins with a **mission statement**.

Here's a dictionary definition of mission: "Purpose, reason for being; an inner calling to perform an activity or a service."

A mission statement is a brief and focused statement of purpose of the direction you want your goals to take you. Using a roadmap as an analogy, the mission statement is the highway you choose to take to get you from where you are to where you want to be, and includes the values (more about values in Chapter 15) with which you make your journey. Goals are the mile markers along the road to your destination. The goals you choose and decisions you make both now and in the future should be based upon your mission statement.

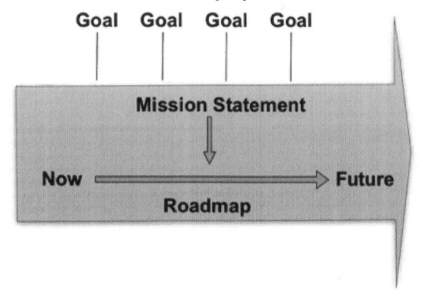

When the mission statement is known, understood, accepted and communicated, positive things happen, and energy and effort are no longer wasted. With it, you will always know whether you are headed in the right direction.

Your personal mission statement will be unlike anyone else's. It will be customized to your unique talents and abilities. In simplest terms, a mission is your most important reason for existence, and vision (more about vision in chapter 13) is what you want to be.

There are **three key properties** your mission statement must include:

1. **Unique**—It must be yours and not anybody else's
2. **Stimulating**—It must stir you into action
3. **Motivating**—It must personally inspire you

Here's the basic structure of a mission statement:

To will/shall use my...(skills, talents)
to..(action)
so that..(result).

A mission statement should be no more than one sentence—usually twenty-five words or less—should be easily understood, and be able to be recited by memory. If you can write one that is short, clear, and resonates with your personal values, then you will have an stimulating mission statement.

—————(Sidebar)—————
Ask the following questions to help find your mission in life.

- What would you like your contribution to be to society?
- What role do you play to achieve your purpose?
- What personal strengths can you add to the world?
- How would you like to be remembered after you die?

Here are some examples. Notice the underlying values, not necessarily spelled out, in these mission statements:

- To use my talents as a mother to coach my children through the early years of their lives so that they can look back on happy, carefree childhoods.
- To use my talents as a writer to write moralistic plays that are entertaining or artistically pleasing so that I'll reach a large audience with my message.
- To create beautiful paintings so that others are inspired by and can enjoy them.
- To use my knowledge and experience as a therapist to aid the regional depression support group so that people with a depression can be helped.
- To use my skills as an architect create magnificent buildings for social gatherings so that people can celebrate in maximum comfort.
- To use my resources as a manager to support others in their work so that the team gets the best results.
- I use my talents and skills as a communicator to publish books and audio with the aim to help people live healthy and happy lives.

Assignment

Now write your own mission statement. Decide what it is you want, and make it clear and specific. This is precisely the purpose of your mission statement. Let this be a labor of love! Pour your heart, mind and soul into it, and if this is your first attempt at writing a mission statement, don't agonize over it. Just get something down. If it doesn't feel right, you can easily change it until it does or come back to it later.

It's useful to review your mission statement every six months. You can add to or alter your mission statement as needed. Place a copy of your mission statement where you can see it daily. It is there to motivate you.

Example: Mission Statement

I use my talents and skills as a communicator to publish self-help books and audio with the aim to help people live healthy and happy lives.

5. Your Vision

You've determined what you wish to achieve and you've written your mission statement, the roadmap that will keep you steady on the right course. You are two important steps closer to getting what you want.

The next step to setting and achieving your goals is your vision statement.

Here's a dictionary definition of vision: "A mental picture of the future we seek to create."

A vision statement describes the detailed mental picture of where you want to see yourself in the future once the mission has been carried out. It may describe how you see events unfolding over ten or twenty years if everything goes exactly as hoped and, like the mission statement, it should be in alignment with your values.

Your vision is to be a reflection of your true core desires. It requires imagination and a positive attitude. Your vision statements projects into the future and creates a desirable picture that motivates and inspires.

- Describes a bright future (hope)
- Describes achievable ambitions
- May include a date or age specification
- Is memorable and engaging
- It's in alignment with your values and beliefs
- It's clear and lacks ambiguity

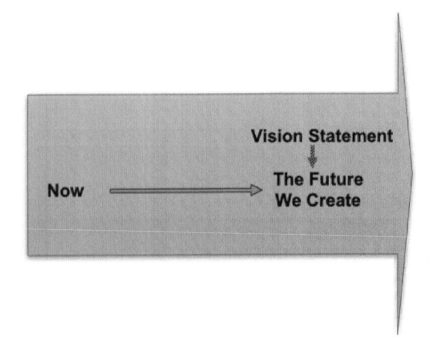

Vision Statement

The Future We Create

Now

What is the difference between a mission and vision statement? If the mission statement is your roadmap, the vision statement is your destination. It's the mental picture of where your mission will take you.

Vision is a long-term view, describing how you would like the world to be in which you live.
A vision statement outlines what you want to be, or how you want the world in which it you live to be. It concentrates on the future. It is a source of inspiration. It provides clear decision-making criteria.

These are some sample vision statements. Again, observe the underlying values:

- When I celebrate my sixtieth birthday, I see many close friends and family enjoying our hospitality. When I enter my study overlooking our beautiful garden, there's a bookshelf filled with several books and CDs with my name on them as author. I feel happy and fulfilled.

- Within the next ten years, I see myself as the top sales rep in my region with a passion for service.
- My vision is that each customer to our store finds the information or material he wants, when he wants it, in the format most fitting for his use.

Assignment

Ready to craft your vision statement? Take the time to create a clear image of the life you want (your vision), then write it down. Remember to include your values, or your vision won't be an accurate reflection of you.

When you have completed your vision, hold that image—focus on it daily. You may opt to rewrite it again and again, and if you do, mix it up a little. Picture yourself in different scenarios enjoying this result. You can add to or alter your vision statement as needed. Place a copy of your vision statement where you can see it daily. Like your mission statement, it is there to inspire you.

—————(Sidebar)—————

Another approach to defining Vision and Mission is to pose two questions. Firstly, "What aspirations do I have for the world in which I live and haves some influence over?", and following on from this, "What can I do or contribute to fulfill those aspirations?". The succinct answer to the first question provides the basis of the Vision Statement. The answer to the second question determines the Mission Statement.

Example: Vision Statement

When I celebrate my sixtieth birthday, I see many close friends and family enjoying our hospitality. When I enter my study overlooking our beautiful garden, there's a bookshelf filled with several books and CDs with my name on them as author. I feel happy and fulfilled.

6. Beliefs

A belief is a experiencing of being sure that someone or something exists or that something is true.

Beliefs are defined as assumptions people make about themselves, about other people and about what makes the world go round.
Beliefs are about how we presume things really are, what we think is really true and what we thus expect as likely consequences that will follow from our actions.
The various ideas you regard as true and use as a solid foundation for daily action!

Beliefs can be both permissive and limiting. Your beliefs and actions that follow based on your beliefs shape your world.
Your chances of success, of reaching what you aim for, go up as soon as you are aware of your own firm beliefs.
Knowing how they affect you can help you put more weight on the beliefs that will support the life you wish for.

Beliefs can be found in broadly spoken, two different flavors.
1. Beliefs as a generalization of reality:
a. "The world is" …", "People are…","Life is", "I am"
2. Beliefs are conditional rules:
a. "If this, then that","If I had won the lottery, I would be rich. " "I have to do everything perfectly all the time to be successful", "In order for me to feel loved, my children must obey me 100 percent of the time without complaint" " if you do good, good will come back threefold"

When a particular person owns a belief, this individual consciously accepts this belief. This can range from mild approval to certain absoluteness.
Consequently it would prove pointless to suggest that a person has these beliefs without them realizing it, or for them to reject their own beliefs.

The phrase "**limiting belief**" is used for a belief that prevents exploration of a wider cognitive space than would otherwise be the case.

A limiting belief holds us back. Illustrations of limiting beliefs can be found in most people. Not many of us our are immune to them. These limiting beliefs might be strongly held beliefs and are often tied in with self-image or perceptions about the world.

Beliefs may be unhealthy or irrational and limiting to us, but we may still be unable to let go of them. Possibly because limiting beliefs existed since we were very young and continued to strengthen over the course of our lives due to self-reinforcing experiences.

Limiting beliefs occur when we form a belief based on incomplete or incorrect information and that belief subsequently limits what we believe to be possible for us. Although we like to think that what we believe to be true really is true, in reality, almost all of us have limiting and false beliefs that negatively effect our life in a variety of ways.

Here are a couple of everyday examples of limiting/self-defeating beliefs:

- That someone has particular capabilities, roles, or traits that can't be changed
- People who're optimistic are not realistic.
- It's a dog-eat-dog world!
- That a specific action or result will be the only method to resolve a certain issue.
- If I'm pleased now, I will not be motivated to alter something in the future.
- I cannot change. This really is simply just the way I am.
- That a specific opinion is correct so there isn't any point thinking about other viewpoints.
- If I control my feelings, I'll be a robot.
- I need love, sex, or money to be happy.
- If I do not really feel guilty about what I did, I'll continue to do bad stuff.
- I can't succeed so there isn't any point to even bother
- No pain, no gain
- If I was pleased all the time, I'd be a complete idiot.
- My feelings come naturally, not something I can control.
- You can't have your cake and eat it too.

- If happiness was my priority, I'd be inconsiderate of other people.

Beliefs are your concept or idea about reality. Beliefs are wide-ranging, and learning where they come from and how they play a role in our life is crucial to begin changing them. Beliefs are the ideas and the concepts we have about who we are and about how the world operates. We have seen some examples of limiting and self-defeating beliefs. Now wouldn't it be great to be able to develop some empowering beliefs then?

How to develop empowering beliefs?
People from around the world agree, the key to success is contained inside you. Your thoughts are your biggest limitation or your strongest asset. You can choose.
Here are five steps to help you develop empowering beliefs or in other words a successful mindset.

1. Recognize your negative thoughts.
Since our life is very much determined by our mind, our thoughts can make or break our life. Every day negative thoughts sneak into our internal language. We say or think things like, "This is a bad day," or "I'm not being very productive," or even, "I'm terrible at ____." These negative thoughts permeate our life and have a strong influence on what we believe deep down. When we say things like, "I'm terrible at saving money," it becomes true. If you give attention to negative thoughts, they will get stronger and stronger! The first step to eliminating negative thoughts is to recognize them. Whenever you have a negative or limiting thought try to pause and reflect on it. Ask questions like:
- Do I really believe this?
- Why am I having this thought?
- Is this a common thought for me?

By stepping back and taking a look at your negative thoughts, you begin to take away their power. It takes practice and patience to recognize them however as you begin to watch your thoughts, you'll become better at catching those negative thoughts before they happen. You can break the vicious cycle by shifting your focus to something positive.

2. Practice positive affirmations.
Another practice which fills your mind, heart and spirit with positive thoughts and helps to drop the negative ones are positive affirmations. A positive affirmation is a statement which, through the act of repetition, becomes implanted in the subconscious mind and influences external forces to manifest this positive change in your life. Affirmations can be created to help you through anything. If for example, you found yourself thinking you are terrible at saving money then a positive affirmation to end that limiting belief might be "I love to save money and am so grateful for the savings I am building." Or "I am masterful with money."

An affirmation practice can be approached in two ways. Many people prefer to recite the affirmation in the morning and throughout the day, making it a practice. While others prefer to use affirmations as a counterbalance to negative thoughts. Thus when they feel themselves thinking negative thoughts about money, for example, they would recite their positive money affirmation.

Affirmation are based on the following principles:
- Your present reality is a direct result of your thinking
- Change your thinking, and your reality changes
- Affirmations change your thinking

Two important beliefs you might want to adopt through affirmations are:
"The past doesn't equal the future"
"There is always a way if I'm committed"

3. Be grateful.
Gratitude may very well be the most positive success tactic available. We often look at what we don't have instead of what we have, and we end up complaining instead of being grateful. It's amazing the calm and peace which comes over you when you feel truly grateful for what you have. When you embrace a practice of gratitude the feeling of "I'll be happy when I'm _____" or "I'll

be successful when I'm _____" goes away and you're allowed to be happy and feel successful right now, today. Now that doesn't mean you can't or shouldn't have goals. Gratitude simply makes it possible to focus on those goals as goals and not needs.

Practicing gratitude can take many forms. Some people find great power in the daily ritual of a gratitude journal. This idea works because it makes recognizing all that you have a daily practice. However, others prefer to tic off what they're grateful for in their head or to simply recognize all they have on an ongoing basis.

Try a **gratitude journal** and see how it changes your life. In a gratitude journal everything you write down must be positive and you can only list something you're grateful for once. So no repeating entries. Look for the positive angle in all things.

4. Recognize success myths.
There are many people who believe success is a combination of luck and hard work. Or who believe that the rich get richer and the poor get poorer. Or that successful people make it because they're in the right place at the right time. What myths about money (You have to pay your dues) and success (nothing comes easy) did you grow up with? What myths do you still hold onto, either consciously or unconsciously?

Spend some time exploring your success myths. Ask yourself what do you believe, why do you believe it and is it really true? You may find that much of what you hold onto as true, you don't really believe, they're just things you picked up as you grew and for one reason or another stuck with you. If you're able to let go of these myths and embrace new beliefs, empowering beliefs about money and success, you will be one step closer to the success you desire. Which brings us to the final step in developing a success mindset: how do you define success?

5. Define success for yourself.
Often when we are asked to define success, we look at those around us who we consider to be successful.

Maybe it's the person down the street with the million dollar home, two new cars in the driveway and a houseful of beautiful well-mannered children or maybe it's the person who owns their own real estate business and is always smiling and wears the best suits.

Additionally, if you pay close attention, we often define success in material forms. "Success is having_____." And we compare what we have to what others have to decide whether we feel successful. Spend some time analyzing your definition for success. Where did it come from? Who do you consider to be successful and why? Then take a look at what you want for your life separate from what others have. You may find that you already fit your personal definition of success. Your definition of success might include having peace of mind, being in good health, spending enough time with your family, or enjoying your job.

Having a successful mindset/empowering beliefs is a prerequisite to living your best life. Embrace these steps, be patient with yourself, they're not easy, and live the successful life you were destined to live.

If you think you have limiting beliefs that could sabotage reaching your goals, and you can't eliminate them by yourself, it would be wise to work on them through counseling.

7. Values

Values are about how we have learnt to think things ought to be or people ought to behave, especially in terms of qualities such as honesty, integrity and openness. Values are traits or qualities that are considered worthwhile; they represent an individual's highest priorities and deeply held driving forces. A value is that for which you make a stand.

Our values determine what goals are significant and what goals will be less important to us. Values go beyond specific actions and circumstances and provide us balance and guidance as we come across hurdles, distractions, opportunities, indecisiveness, ambivalence, turmoil, and temptations throughout our lives.

Your values are based on your beliefs.

What do values have to do with goal setting?
Simply this. If the goals you set are out of alignment with your values, it will make those goals extremely difficult to achieve. For instance, if you value integrity, it probably wouldn't be wise to want to become the most successful hard-selling door-to-door salesperson of useless products.

The step of defining your values is important; effective people identify and develop a clear, concise and understood meaning of their values. Once defined, values impact every aspect of your choices, work behavior, interpersonal interaction, contributions, and the goals you set.

You might hold different values for work and for your private life. But as the lines between your professional and personal lives become less defined, it's important that you create symmetry and provide balance between both so that, as much as circumstances allow, you can be yourself. If you can't be you, how can you be happy?

Means values are helpful values (money, business success) in that they are required as part of the effort to achieve other values.

Ends values (like love, happiness, accomplishment, security, adventure) are both more general and more important in driving all of our behaviors as human beings. Example: I need money (means value) to feel secure (end value).

Values are generally sorted hierarchically.

Following are some examples of values. You might use these as the starting point for introspection into your own values.
They could be the answer to one of the following questions:
- What's important to me about my life?
- What's important to me about my family?
- What's important to me about my career?

I value:
- Acceptance
- Accountability
- Accuracy
- Achievement
- Adventure
- Affection
- Ambition
- Appreciation
- Authenticity
- Balance
- Beauty
- Belonging
- Benevolence
- Camaraderie
- Care
- Career
- Certainty
- Challenge
- Collaboration
- Commitment
- Comfort

- Compassion / Love
- Competence
- Competition
- Conformity
- Confidence
- Connection
- Contribution
- Courage
- Creativity
- Credibility
- Curiosity
- Decisiveness
- Dedication
- Dependability
- Development
- Devotion
- Dignity
- Discipline
- Effectiveness
- Efficiency
- Empathy
- Empowerment
- Enthusiasm
- Excellence
- Excitement
- Fairness
- Faith
- Family
- Financial Independence
- Flexibility
- Forgiveness
- Freedom
- Friendliness
- Friendship
- Fun
- Generosity

- Genuineness
- Gratitude
- Growth
- Happiness
- Harmony
- Health
- Hedonism
- Honesty
- Honor
- Humanity
- Humility
- Humor
- Independence
- Influence
- Innovativeness
- Inspiration
- Integrity
- Intuition
- Involvement
- Joy
- Justice
- Kindness
- Knowledge
- Leadership
- Learning
- Love / Compassion
- Loyalty
- Moderation
- Money
- Nature
- Openness
- Order
- Partnership
- Passion
- Patience
- Peace of Mind

- Perseverance
- Persistency
- Play
- Pleasure
- Power
- Prestige
- Quality
- Recognition
- Reflection
- Respectfulness
- Respect for life
- Responsibility
- Security
- Self-restraint
- Serenity
- Service
- Significance
- Sincerity
- Spirituality
- Stability
- Status
- Success
- Teamwork
- Tolerance
- Tradition
- Trust
- Truthfulness
- Uncertainty
- Unity
- Variety
- Wealth
- Wisdom

─────────(Sidebar)─────────

When your values are in conflict, internal challenges may emerge. Chances are you will end up with competing values

Define which values you consider non-negotiable that no matter what will not be sacrificed to any other values. Creating a list of non-negotiables helps prioritize values in instances where there is conflict.

Assignment

List your personal values (My Personal Values). If you have difficulty determining them, ask yourself, "What's most important to me in life?" until you run out of answers.

Then, sort them by the importance you give them from say 1 to 10, where 1 is your most prominent value and 10 is the least. Next to each of your values you jot down reasons why you've chosen this particular value.

To help you find out which values are most important to you, establish a hierarchy by asking yourself, "What's more important for me to feel: _____ or ____ ?"

For example, you can say, "I have chosen recognition as my number one value because I don't want to live a life anonymously," or, "I have settled creativity as my number two value because I want to add creativity to everything that I do."

————————(Sidebar)————————

Pick the particular five to ten keywords that describe what is most important to you. Thoroughly examine and introduce verbs as appropriate in each values statement to make it effective, precise, and meaningful to you.

For example, the value "Security" may become "Safety for loved ones","protection of my country" from enemies, "Stability of society", 'Avoidance of indebtedness", or some other phrase that more precisely describes your particular values. Ask close friends if this list of values agrees with how they see you.

Values as well as their order of importance are strictly personal.

Next, see if you can group them according to common themes-you will likely discover a mere handful of values govern your existence. Examples of common themes are:

- Personal Development and Self Awareness
- Equity and Equality
- Interpersonal Communication
- Community and Social Development & Responsibility
- Health and Well Being
- Leadership
- Love and Friendship
- Accountability and Work Responsibility
- Team Development and Collaboration

Great. You made stock of the values that are important to you and tried to find clusters of values that pop up often. Look over your values and their hierarchy once more. If, for example, dependability, friendliness, and loyalty tops your list, that may suggest working with others is of higher value to you than working alone.

Values are what makes you unique. They form your purposes in life. They are your priorities. They are the fuel that will propel you forward.

If you truly value your time and money then you won't waste it on things you don't want to do and on things you don't truly love and value. It's really that simple.

With the insight your list provides, you can be sure to set goals in alignment with those values. That will make your goals easier to achieve. If what you do (the "outside") is in harmony or in alignment with the values you deem important (your "inside") you will be able to live a happier, more peaceful, and purposeful life. You will notice the goals you set are a means and not an end.

By adhering to a system of clearly defined personal values you will have a clear conscience and a clear purpose in everything you do.

Example: My Personal Values

- Accountability
- ~~Certainty~~
- Security
- Creativity
- Enthusiasm
- ~~Significance~~
- Self Restraint

8. Beliefs and Values

"We are what we think," said Buddha.

A person's goals have to be supported and justified by a persons beliefs and values.

Is there a difference between a belief and a value? There is no simple answer. Though there are similarities, there are actually some differences between them too. Beliefs and values are closely related. They cannot be seen separate from each other. In essence, beliefs provide context for values. They are more or less interrelated.

Both beliefs and values influence the way we see ourselves. They also serve as filters for our understanding of the world around us.

Probably the biggest difference is that our values usually change more over time than our beliefs. Each stage of our life requires adjustments and will also cause us to reevaluate our values. On the other hand, our beliefs are not likely to change as often. Our lifestyles may change, but the ideas we hold as true will generally remain the same. It will take some strong "evidence" to dent our beliefs.

Belief is a sense of being sure that someone or something exists or that something is true.
Something regarded as true.

Though others may dispute their believability, if someone sincerely believes in a feeling or cause, it can be recognized as a personal belief.

Your beliefs sort and filter data in order to prove themselves to be true. Beliefs are priceless generalizations that people use to give themselves a sense of certainty and a basis for decision-making in an uncertain and unpredictable world.

Value is a strongly held opinion about what is valuable, important, or acceptable.

Something held in high regard.

Values are based on beliefs.

We hold something in high regard, because we regard it as true.

Thus what you believe determines what you deem valuable.

Beliefs are basically things we take for granted about ourselves, about others in the world and about how we believe things to be. They are usually half-truths. Beliefs are about how we think things truly are and what we think is certainly true. A typical belief may be "stealing is wrong." A belief includes not only an action or activity ("stealing"), but also a judgment about that action or activity ("is wrong").

Our values are based on our beliefs. A value is something that we consider to be important and meaningful and can include specific ideas, behaviors, attitudes, relationships and concepts like "equality, liberty, honesty, knowledge, education, obedience, charity, truthfulness, effort, privacy, perseverance, integrity, loyalty, solidarity & faithfulness". Values govern how we interact with the world.

Our motivation and behavior is heavily influenced by our values. Values are abstract and hierarchical concepts that essentially describe what we want to achieve. Holding a value means we aspire to something, or we feel that value is worth something to us. So if we say that we hold "loyalty" as a value we are saying that we aspire to be loyal, even at personal cost.

It is imaginable for our beliefs and values to change over time as we gather evidence or have experiences that defy our previously held views. On the other hand our beliefs and values can also be reinforced by experience or evidence.

Everyone has a system of beliefs and values that they have developed during their lives.

To sum it up beliefs are judgments that give our experiences meaning, and provide a context for our values.

While personal values are undeniably woven into personal beliefs, values are personal choices that are seldom discussed, because they help define our individuality.

PART TWO: Goal Setting

9. Goal Setting

The best opportunities offered to you in life are often the ones you create yourself.
Without a force or action imposed on an object, no motion or movement can take place. The same is true with your life.

In order to achieve goals, it is imperative that you act yourself.

But how can you do so effectively?
Well, there is one major and significant key -- goal setting.

Setting personal or business goals is the key to success.
Our ambitions give us focus. They enable us to focus our attention, energy and resources on issues that matter most rather than allowing us to become distracted by the things that don't.

Goals expand our possibilities.
With goals, we can greatly improve ourselves. Create fresh boundaries, set new records and accomplish great things.

Your time and energy are exceedingly precious, so it's better to invest a little portion of time to arrange the right goals. You don't wish to waste your efforts on ill set goals and wind up crying over spilled milk after discovering you've spent your time in vain.

Goal setting requires self-discipline, time and effort, which is something only a small percentage of people will discipline themselves to do.

As a result, many people will either never begin the process of goal setting, or give up on their goals before they complete them.
Setting (personal) goals requires you to take some time out and actively think about what you want to accomplish in life.
Goal setting is therefore not something that you can just read about.
Goal setting is something you must physically do.

There are all kinds of goals you can create. Some goals are short-term, others are long-term. Some goals are easily understood whilst others can become subject of to much interpretation. Some goals are effortlessly accomplished, but others are impossible to attain.

—————————(Sidebar)—————————
If you are interested in other people's goals you are invited to take a peek on the 43things.com website at
http://www.43things.com/zeitgeist/goals
In fact, looking at other people's goals might get you inspired!
—————————————————

10. SMART Goals

A goal is an action statement. So start it with a verb. Like increasing or reducing. You are trying to change something. It's designed for movement so use action words like increase, decrease, build, direct, organize, read, develop etcetera. For instance.

I want to increase customer satisfaction with 10% by January 2014

SMART is a handy acronym often used to develop goals. SMART stands for: Specific, Measurable, Actionable (Achievable), Realistic and Time bound). It has proven to work in theory and more importantly in practice. Keep in mind however that there is no clear consensus about what the five keywords mean, or even what they are in any given situation.

Specific

Goals should be Specific in terms of behaviors or specific events. "Being happy," for example, is neither an event nor a behavior. When you set out to identify a goal, define what you want in clear and specific terms of operations, meaning what has to be done. When a goal is divided into small steps, it can be handled and attacked much more directly.

Is it specific enough that anyone would know the next step.

They should tell us what exactly is expected, when and how much. They must be clear and unambiguous. They have a starting point and ending point.

- What are you going to do.
- Why is this important to do?
- How are you going to do it?
- Who: Who is involved?
- Where: Identify a location.
- Which: Identify requirements and constraints.
- When: identify a time frame.

Measurable

Goals should be Measurable.

How else are you going to be capable to figure out your level of progress, or know if you have successfully arrived where you dreamed of being? To be able to tell whether or not you are getting closer to reaching your goals you should attach specific 'numbers' to them. They ought to have numbers, such as: "I will make 6 sales this month" or "I will increase my revenue by 15% by the end of 2013." If your goal is simply to "increase revenue," that is not measurable. 'I want to spend 8 more hours a week with my family' is an example of a goal with life changing power. It is specific, identifiable, and measurable. You in fact will be able to know the exact moment this goal is reached.

- How do you measure your success?
- What does success look like?
- How would you know that you reached your goal.

If you can't measure it, you can't manage it. So choose a goal with measurable progress, so you can notice the change occur.
You should be able to measure whether you are meeting the objectives or not.

So establish concrete criteria for measuring progress towards attainment of each goal. When you measure progress, you stay on track, reach your target dates, and experience the exhilaration of achievement that spurs you onto continued effort required to reach your goal.
A measurable goal will usually answer questions such as:

- How much?
- How many?
- How will I know when it is accomplished?

Actionable/Achievable
Goals should be Attainable.
Make sure your goals are only slightly out of your reach, opposed to 'a promise of heaven'. Goals are a tool to help you achieve success, they are not meant to be pipe-dreams. Improving your paycheck 500% in the next year for example could be an example of an unattainable. On the other hand getting a 10% raise, for instance, may be very realistic.

An attainable goal will usually answer the question "How can the goal be accomplished". But whatever you decide to accomplish, your goals should be set toward the top of what is possible. At the same time don't be too hard on yourself, if you don't always make it all the way to your goal. In fact if you always easily meet your goals you aren't setting them high enough.

Actionable implies that when you read it over a year you still know what has to be done.
- How are you going to reach it.
- Is it something you can do?
- Will you be able to reach your goal?
- Can you break it into actionable steps?

Realistic / Relevant
Goals should be Relevant.
This means, you are willing to reach that goal (because it is worthwhile and you are the right person to pursue it) and are able to do so under your current circumstances. Doing so propels you to higher levels and helps you achieve more successes in life.

Do some research to find out if your goal is realistic.
Goals that are too far out of your reach won't motivate you. Even though you might start with the best of intentions the knowledge that your goal is just to much for you will keep you from even giving it your best.

A goal needs to stretch you slightly to keep you motivated. Realistic means "do-able". Be sure to set goals that you can attain with some effort! Set the bar high enough for a satisfying achievement.
Too difficult sets the stage for failure. Too easy sends the message that you are not very able. Be real and honest.
- Can you realistically achieve the objectives with the resources you have?
- Does this goal fit in with other goals & life plans.
- Is the goal in alignment with who you are.
- Does this seem worthwhile?

- Is this the right time?
- Does this match your other efforts/needs?
- Is it congruent.

Time Bound / Trackable
Goals should be Timely.
Be sure your goal has a specific deadline. Not 'someday' but rather a specific date. The point is that they must be timely. This also anchors them within a timeframe. Otherwise, you are setting yourself up for failure.

Set a deadline for your goal. Without a time limit, there's no urgency to start taking action now. Your deadline must also be realistic of course.
- When should the goal be completed?
- A goal must have a starting point, ending point and fixed durations.

I am going to try to lift weight is a bad goal. (try, could, should, possible could do, soon, by the end of the year)

I will bench press 5 repetitions of 200 lbs by the end of December.

Goals should be easily defined in terms of steps. Steady advance, through well-chosen, sensible, interval steps, delivers results in the end. Determine what those steps are before beginning.

In addition to the points mentioned in the previous section on the SMART acronym you might want to consider the following too.

Goals should be accountable for.
Without accountability, people are likely to con themselves. Once you know exactly what you want, when you want it — and there are serious consequences for not doing the designated work — you are even more likely to continue in your pursuit of your goal.

Ask somebody inside your circle of friends and family to whom you can be accountable. Ask this person for periodic feedback on the reports on your progress

Goals should be Visible.
Make a list of your goals, and put them somewhere you will see them at least daily.

Setting SMART Goals is is one of the best thing you can do to make your venture a success.

Spending some time upfront defining your goals can save you a lot of frustration and disappointment further down the road.

SMART goals are easier to craft than control.
So keep your goals in sight!

If you add **E** (**ecology** of the goal) and **R** (**reward** of the goal) to make them SMARTER you more or less have a 'well formed outcome'. We'll talk more about that in the next chapter.

11. Well Formed Outcomes

Neuro-Linguistic Programming (NLP) was developed in 1975 and focuses on learning how to think and feel without judgment. Among many other things it teaches people how to free themselves from unwanted desires and bad habits.

One important part of NLP is goal setting. In order to achieve this, NLP has created goal setting criteria called the well-formed outcome model. This model offers a way for followers to test their goals in order to see if they are truly attainable and to learn how they can be achieved. NLP teaches that goal setting is the first step in becoming a successful person both individually, and in relationships. The NLP goal model works by making goals specific to certain senses in the body. This specificity directs your attention to what you already see, feel and hear internally. You will then link your internal and external forces together in order to attain your goals in an effective way. By combining your internal and external forces, you can move from your present state to a state you never thought possible.

The **well-formed outcome model** is a way to refine goals and clarify what exactly it is that you want and what you truly hope to get out of setting your goal.

The term well-formed simply means that your goal has passed through the well-formed outcome model, and is an achievable goal. If a goal does not pass through the model, then the goal is likely unattainable, and it would be unrealistic to ever achieve said goal. The well-formed outcome model is comprised of seven questions/categories that allow its users to truly think about the parameters of their goal and decide for themselves if they can accomplish their goal, and if so, how they can go about accomplishing and maintaining their goal.

These questions are what comprises the well-formed outcome model.

1. Can you state your goal in positive terms?

While stating your goal in positive terms take into account what your present state is. Then, determine if your desired state is better or worse than your present state, if worse, then abandon your goal, or reassess your goal to make it a positive thing. Think about how you can go about achieving your goal in a positive way. Also, state what you want to achieve and what you are working towards.

2. Can you state your goal in sensory based terms?

State your goal in sensory terms. Think about what you will see, hear, think and feel when you will achieve your goal. Think about the senses in terms of achieving your goal so that you can engage all of your senses in achieving your goal. Also, think about whether or not you have dissected your goal into enough small steps so that each step is achievable and won't overwhelm your senses.

3. How is the goal compelling to you? (Reward)

Is your goal exciting? Do you have a passion to complete your goal? If the answer is yes, then you are on the right track to completing your goal in the future. Make your goal sound compelling, so that you can imagine yourself and your life after you have accomplished the goal you set.

4. Does the goal suit you in every aspect of your life? (Ecology)

Will your goal fit into every nook and cranny of your life? Will it be harmful or helpful to your relationships and yourself? Make sure that your goal fits into every part of your life, even the small parts, so that once you achieve your goal you won't have to confine your ideas to fit into certain parts of your life.

5. Can you initiate the goal yourself, and maintain it yourself?

Self-initiated goals are ones that you will be able to maintain in the long run. Test your goal to be certain that it is within your power to do. If your goal is not self-initiated and it is dependent on other people's actions then it will not be accomplished or maintained easily.

6. What is the context of your goal?

Think about your goal and how you can accomplish your goal, with who you will need to talk to in order to accomplish said goal, where you will need to go to accomplish said goal, etc. Contextualize your goal and be certain that it is realistic.

7. What resources will you need to complete your goal?

Determine the resources that you will need in order to attain your goal. Resources can include other people, certain material items or even something as simple as free time. Make a list of the resources that you'll need so that you can go back and read this list when you are feeling less than eager to keep working towards your goal.

The well-formed outcome method is a method that involves testing your goals against the well-formed outcome model in order to determine if your goal is attainable. Goal setting is an important part of the human experience, and in order to be a successful person in your own life and in relationships, it is pertinent to have well-formed goals in your life.

12. Goal Setting Model

In the next 5 chapters I'll walk you through a goal setting model involving Who, Why, How, What, Where, When and With Whom.

The fact that all items touch every other item is consistent with the view that any change in one element may, if necessary, trigger changes in other parts of the goal setting model.
The model places the elements (Who, Why, How, What) within a context (Where, When and With Whom).

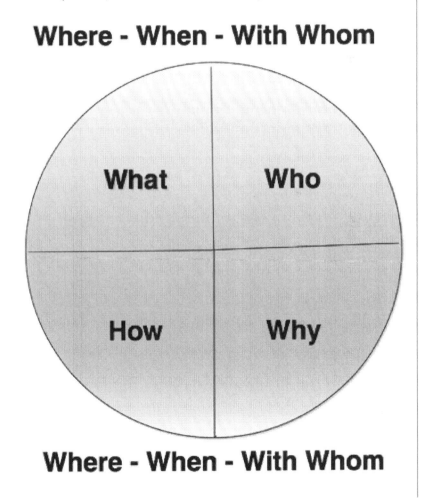

This model is useful for assisting with or understanding goal setting from an individual or organization point of view.

According to the model, the items influence each other in all directions.

When we walk through the different items of this model (see the figure below) keep in mind that all items are strongly related to each other (see figure above).

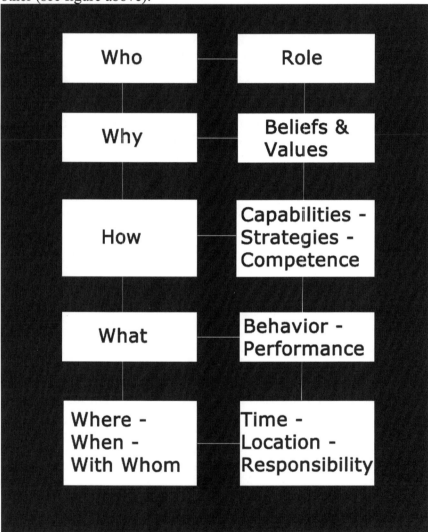

It may seem obvious that all the different parts of your life are deeply interconnected. But a common way to treat problems is to try to isolate them. If there's a problem with your health, you need to diet and exercise. If there's a problem in your career, it's time to work harder. But this isolation protocol doesn't work well because there's too much overlap between all the different parts of your life, no matter how much you try to isolate the problem areas and go to work on them.

It's often the case that the obvious cause of the problem isn't the true source. If you feel lonely because you haven't been able to find the right relationship, and you keep trying harder and harder to find a relationship, you may get nowhere.

The problem may be that you work at a career you are not passionate about, and you project this lack of passion to everyone you meet. And still a deeper issue may be that your spiritual beliefs tell you that service to others is very important, but you don't feel you are doing that. Then you change careers to do what you love, and it aligns with your spiritual beliefs because now you feel you are contributing and serving. Then out of nowhere, you meet your future spouse, who is attracted to your passion about your work and the contribution you are making. And the encouragement you experience from this relationship in turn helps you advance your career, increase your income, and free up more time to spend with your new spouse. Your stress goes down, and your health improves too. Your inner spiritual conflict was the real source of your inability to find the right relationship. Everything is deeply interconnected.

This model (loosely based on The NLP Logical Levels of Change Model, inspired by Gregory Bateson and developed by Robert Dilts) can help you plan goals that are in alignment with your environment, behaviors, competencies, beliefs/values, and identity.

13. Goal Setting: Who

You've listed goals and things about yourself or your life you wish to improve in order of their importance to you. You've penned your mission statement—the roadmap you've chosen to follow—and your vision statement—your end result (how you view your future success and happiness).

When you work through the following chapters keep in mind that Goals are there to bring purpose and meaning to your life. You will find success in the journey to your goal. It's all about bringing passion (back) to your life. Success does not merely follow after goals have been accomplished but they occur during the process of working towards their completion.

Goals should identify a specific outcome and should answer the six W's. In the next chapters we will explore six components to consider whenever setting a goal:
A Specific goal will usually answer these questions:
- Who (Chapter 22)
- Why (Chapter 23)
- How (Chapter 24)
- What (Chapter 25)
- Where, When and With Whom (Chapter 26)

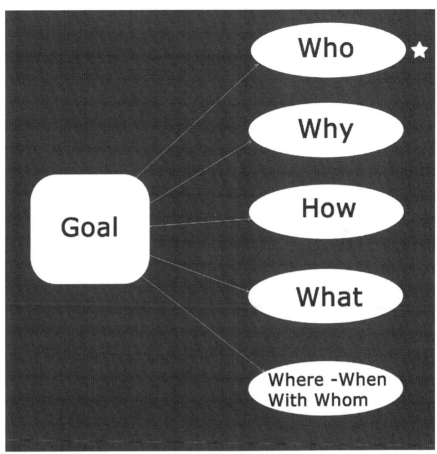

Who? Who are you as an individual?

First, "Who."

Who is the person setting the goal? You, of course. What role do you play to achieve your purpose? Who are you or what role do you play? Is it the role necessary to achieve your purpose? What do you need to change?

When you take a close look at yourself and take note of your actions and thoughts during a day, you probably think of yourself as a pretty good actor, an actor who acts according to a script, and an actor with enormous improvising qualities matching the different demands that meet him/her all the time. This actor in us can manage a vast amount of roles.

All through life, you play different roles depending on what you are doing and to whom you are relating. For example, when you are talking with your parents your role is son or daughter, but when you are talking to your children your role is father or mother. At work you may at various times be a manager, a subordinate, a coworker. At other times you may be a trusted friend, a volunteer and so on.

Classifying your role is one of the five components that enables you to set a clear goal. Here are examples of different roles:

- father
- mother
- husband
- wife
- son
- daughter
- brother
- sister
- grandfather
- grandmother
- boyfriend
- girlfriend
- income provider
- volunteer
- boss
- employee
- project leader
- team member
- mentor
- student
- sportsman/woman
- friend
- neighbor
- salesman
- writer

Which role will you play to achieve each of your goals?

Assignment

Now write: "Who" followed by the role you will play as you set out to achieve your goals. For each goal a unique role.

—————(Sidebar)—————

If you have more than 7 "Areas of Responsibility" [Roles] on your plate you are most likely spreading yourself too thin.

Here are the roles I defined for myself in this moment of time.

- Author
- Husband
- Father
- Son
- Social media enthusiast
- Treasurer
- Traveler

Anything outside of that is just for fun or distraction. The fact is that you can only focus on so much, and that has to be devoted to what you regard as really important. If you remove all the unimportant bits and pieces in your life you might get some more meaningful work done.

14. Goal Setting: Why

The second component to consider whenever setting a goal is
"Why."

Why do you want to achieve an objective? Why do you do
something? What do you believe in or value? Most likely the answer
is because you believe in or value that objective.

What beliefs do you have about yourself, about others, about the
world in general? Do these beliefs support you in fulfilling your role
(Who: Chapter 22)? What do you value - in yourself, others, the
world in general? Are these values in alignment with your role? Are
there other beliefs and values that you could take on that would be
more in alignment?

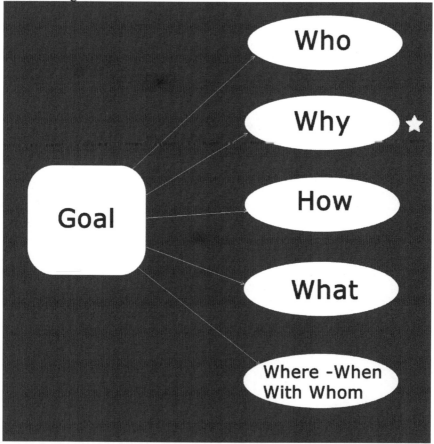

Finding your "Why" means finding your purpose, what drives you, what you are truly passionate about. Many people fail at achieving success simply because they lack clear motives for doing so.

Incorporating the "Why" into your goals will enable you to achieve them while enjoying the steps you will take along the way.

Even the drudgery we sometimes have to deal with is easier to manage if we know why we must do it. Understanding "Why" will make necessary tasks a part of your plan, and thus a choice rather than a load.

Explain to yourself why you want to achieve this goal. What happened for you to want this, and how it will change your life. The more compelling your motives and reasons are, the greater the odds are that you will accomplish your goals. Conversely, if you can't come up with "good" reasons, you might as well move on to another goal, as this one won't be achieved.

Do you want $5 million at retirement? Why? You say you want to live in a mansion? Why? You want that new car? Why?
There are no wrong answers here. "Whys" are the principles, standards, or qualities considered worthwhile or desirable by the person (or couple or family or team) who holds them. What one person or group thinks is stupid or vain, another will think is great or worthy. You need to come up with benefits that are honest, powerful and inspiring to you or your group. And the more "Whys" you have for each objective, the better.

Here is an example of "Why":
I want to reach my goal (become senior account manager) because I believe it is important for me to stay financially secure. And I value a career and feel responsible for maintaining a good income for my family.

Think about how you feel as achieve your goal. What can you see, smell and hear? Are you excited, nervous, relieved?

You can also view "Whys," simply, as the list of benefits to you for reaching this goal.

For example, benefits for a fitness goal might include feeling great, clothes fit well and look good, and people compliment me.

If you have strong enough "Whys" for your goals, you are going to pursue your goals until you achieve them. Not achieving them would give you more pain than doing what needs to be done in order to realize your goals.

Assignment

Give serious thought why you want to achieve each of your objectives. Beneath each "Who," write: "Why" followed by your reasons for wanting to achieve that objective, or simply write a list of benefits.

Review your "Whys" monthly, making adjustments when necessary, and you will find yourself becoming more motivated to strive toward your goals.

15. Goal Setting: How

The third component to consider whenever setting a goal is **"How."** "How" are you going to achieve your objective? How? How do you go about doing things?

What capabilities/strategies/action plans do you have? Do you need to develop new capabilities, strategies or action plans? Are they in alignment with the Why (chapter 23) and the Who (chapter 22) ? If not, what needs to be changed? Perhaps you need to change your capabilities (get more training), your strategies or action plans. Or maybe, given this new information, you need to reassess your role (Who) or your beliefs and values (Why).

To be able to do so, you must have the necessary **strategy and resources** in place.

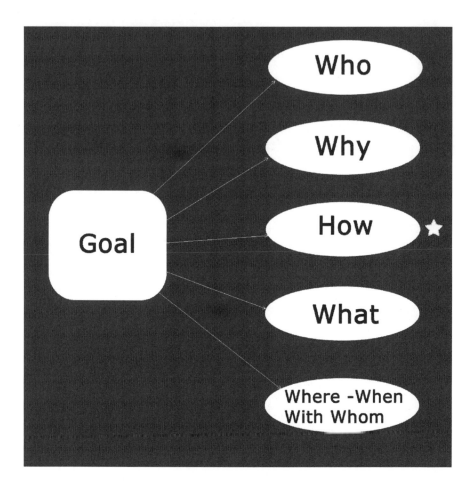

Capabilities/Strategies/Competence/Skills

As a simple definition, "strategy" is the specific steps it will take to reach your goal.

For example, let's say your goal is this: "I want to go back to school and get a bachelor's degree in English by December 31st of next year." That's a decent goal, but you aren't just going to walk onto a college campus and be awarded a degree in English. You must determine which school to attend, how to pay for school, and how many classes to take at one time, among other details. There must be a strategy.

Let's take strategy even further, again considering the college goal. Earning the degree itself is a pretty big goal. "How" are you going to achieve your objective? You can break it down into smaller goals.

For instance, one of those smaller goals could be: "I want to finish four classes by the end of this year."

A goal may be short term, medium term or long term. Some people call everything under a week "short term," under six months "medium term," and over six months "long term." Others might choose different time frames.

Short-term goals are ones that you will achieve soon, such as within a day, within a week, or possibly within a few months. They are often the stepping-stones that lead up to medium- and long-term goals, and are a great way to progress through your plan. Those stepping-stones are your strategy. Short-term goals keep you from becoming overwhelmed or losing sight of your long-term goal. They give you steps to look forward to so that you can celebrate along the way to the larger goal.

What you decide you want to accomplish by next week, and where you decide you want to be in one year, or five, or even twenty, will have an impact on what you do today. Be ready to plan your strategy.

Assignment
Consider the goals you've written down. Write "short-term" next to each short-term objective, "medium-term" next to each medium-term objective, and "long-term" next to each long-term objective. By doing so, you are beginning to plan your strategy, or the steps (short-term goals) you will take to reach those goals, to get you from here to there.

For instance—using our roadmap analogy and an imagined scenario to go with it—let's say you want to drive from San Francisco to San Diego (that's your long-term goal). Your "Who" is "nephew," because you're driving to San Diego to see your uncle. Your "What" of course, is to arrive in San Diego. Your "Why" is because he adores you and he just won the lottery. Now, for such a long drive, it helps to make stops (short-term goals) along the way. Your first goal can be to get to San Jose. Your next goal will be to get to the 5 Freeway. And so on.

The short-term goals need to be arranged one behind the other, in the order they need to be accomplished in order to achieve the bigger objective. These new short-term goals will be your strategy.

Resources
The other important aspect of determining "How" a goal will be carried out is the resources you have available, or will have available, to achieve that goal.

Resources are necessary to carry out a task. They usually are people, equipment, facilities, funding, or anything else capable of or required for completing a goal.

An assistant is a resource, more education is a resource, and an encouraging mate is a resource. Other resources may include books, tapes, seminars you would like to attend, courses you would like to complete, mentors, and coaches.

A list of your resources is a valuable tool for making and accomplishing goals because you can instantly draw on resources to help you. If you don't currently have a certain, necessary resource available to you, you will need to determine when you will get it and how it will be obtained.

"How" are you going to achieve your objective using resources?

What is it you want to accomplish? If you want to start your own business in the next couple of years, then you know you have to set back cash (resource) to obtain this goal. You will also need to decide if you need extra skills (resource) or education (resource) to set up the business. Here you'll notice that resources and strategy go hand-in-hand. Resources are those people or items capable of or required for completing a goal. The actual planning of what you'll need and determining the steps you'll take to achieve them is strategy. Let's assume I planned to become a senior account manager.
Consequently, I will volunteer to perform chores (strategy) with a friend of mine who is a senior account manager at another company, and while performing those chores, I'll ask him for some useful tips (resources).

The most important resource you have is . . . Guess who? . . . Yourself.

You might like to do what marketing consultants call a SWOT on yourself—this is where you analyze your Strengths, Weaknesses, Opportunities and Threats.

You'll probably only want to put your strengths and opportunities in your resources list. Think about your abilities—physically, mentally, and in terms of confidence. Your strengths and achievements in these areas are good resources for you to draw on.

Assignment

In your journal, beneath each "Why," write: "How: Resources Currently Available." List every resource you currently have available to you in terms of your own experience and outside resources.

Now, beneath each "How: Resources Currently Available," write: "How: Resources I Will Need to Obtain." List every resource you can think of that you currently do not have available but will need to obtain. Leave space to add to this list as further thoughts or ideas for resources surface.

As additional thoughts or ideas for resources surface, make and arrange new objectives—and the "Who" and "Why"—needed to obtain their resource objectives.

Review and adjust the resources you need to obtain and the strategy needed to carry out the "How" regularly.

16. Goal Setting: What

The fourth component to consider whenever setting a goal is **"What."**

What? **What are your behaviors?** What you do and how you behave. Our behavior is made up of the specific actions we take within our environment.

What do people really see/experience in your behaviors? Are your behaviors in alignment with Who, Why and How? Does something need to be changed?

Simply put, "What" is your goal, written in the framework of a performance rather than an outcome.

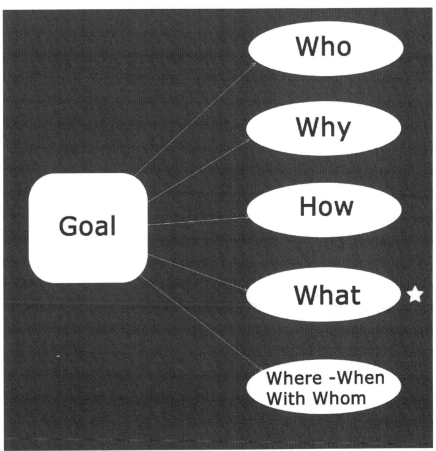

 When thinking about what your goal is, you need to think of it in terms of a way of getting the result that you want, not as the actual outcome that you're hoping to achieve.

Just think about it for a moment. How much of a 'final goal' can you control, without the influence of other people or events? An athlete may train with a goal to win an Olympic gold medal, and hit all of their performance targets along the way, but, in the actual race, the end goal that they set from the start could be taken away from them by a better athlete, or some mistake that they make during their event.

Having an outcome as a goal has too many variables that you cannot control, meaning your goal is often unachievable. To succeed in achieving an outcome orientated goal you have to be able to take into account the things that could go wrong, and find a way to overcome them if they do. Also, you have to always be better than anyone else who may be standing in the way of you reaching that goal - and allowing for the skills and strengths of other people is much more difficult.

Failing to reach an outcome goal is easier to take if it's due to outside influences, than it is if it's simply down to you not being prepared enough, or just not being capable of reaching that final goal.

Another problem with outcome goals is the fact that they are generally based on you receiving some form of reward when you achieve your goal. Although the reward may sound very tempting when you first start out, it can begin to sound a lot less appealing if you aren't going to receive that reward for some months; furthermore, as mentioned earlier, there is no guarantee that you will reach that final goal anyway, so the thought of the reward can become less motivating over the following days, weeks, months, or even years. When that starts to happen, you give up, and never get anywhere near reaching the goal that you have set.

Of course, if your goals are more achievable, and lead on to further goals on your path to improving your performance or knowledge, then you are going to be able to stay focused, reach each new goal along the way, and feel good about having done it. If you do need to have an outcome goal, then using these 'progress goals' to help you along the way is going to see you reach your outcome, without the doubts and lack of focus that you may have otherwise had along the way.

In the athletic event example: if you get disqualified in the early heats, or you are simply beaten by three or more athletes who are better than you, then you are not going to achieve your aim of getting into the finals, and ultimately winning that gold medal. If, on the other hand, your aim was to beat a personal best, and you achieve that without going any further in the competition, then it's not a total loss. You may not be in with a chance to win gold, but you will have the satisfaction of reaching the goal you had set, and that may be enough for you to build on in future events.

Before you try to reach for something that you may have no hope of achieving, stop to think for a moment. Who are you trying to do this for? What are you trying to do? Is it an outcome goal, or a progress goal? So, take some time to write down something that you want to achieve for yourself, and make sure that it is something that is realistic. If it's personal enough, realistic enough and it will make you happy, then it is achievable; who knows, maybe later you can try to take the next big step using the goal setting skills that you are starting to perfect.

Assignment
Beneath each "Who,""Why"and "How" write: "What." Then rewrite the dream or aspect of yourself you wish to set a goal to achieve, in the framework of a performance.

Often whenever you start formulating a goal, it can help to jot it down as if your goal has already been achieved. Your goal should be something that you genuinely desire. Not your spouse's, not your father's, not what you think someone else wants of you. These goals should be tied directly to what you want, to what makes you happy. What you feel passionate about.

17. Goal Setting: Where, When & With Whom (The Context)

The final components to consider whenever setting a goal are **"When, Where and with whom"**

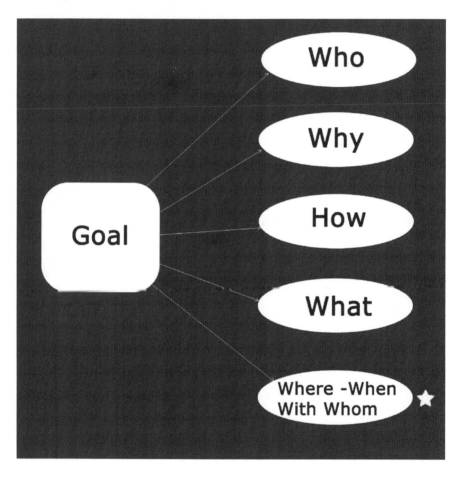

All goals must have deadlines because it's a psychological law that work always expands to fill the time allowed. So goals we set must have target dates, time frames for completion.

Set a timeframe for the goal: for next week, in three months, by fifth grade. Putting an end point on your goal gives you a clear target to work towards.

If you don't set a time, the commitment is too vague. It tends not to happen because you feel you can start at any time. Without a time limit, there's no urgency to start taking action now.

For example, many of us may want to find a new job or start our own business.
We spend a lot of time talking about what we want to do, someday. But without an end date, there is no sense of urgency, no reason to take any action today.
Having a specific time frame, a "When," gives you the impetus to get started.
It also helps you check your progress.

The **"where"** is usually the simple part. You need to Identify a location. Where do you achieve your goal. Start with the future environment in which you want to achieve the goal. This is a creative exercise, there are no limits! Choose the nicest offices or houses, in which you really would love to work or live. If that is applicable in the context of your goal setting. Working towards a goal often implies making a change in one's environment; it could involve bringing in an organizational specialist to rearrange an office environment in support of a mission or job, or it could be as simple as reorganizing furniture, adjusting the temperature or making ergonomic changes.

The person(s) involved in helping you reach a goal fall into the **"With Whom"** section.

Assignment
Beneath each "How," write: "When" followed by the date you want to accomplish that objective, Where and With Whom.

18. Write Your Goals

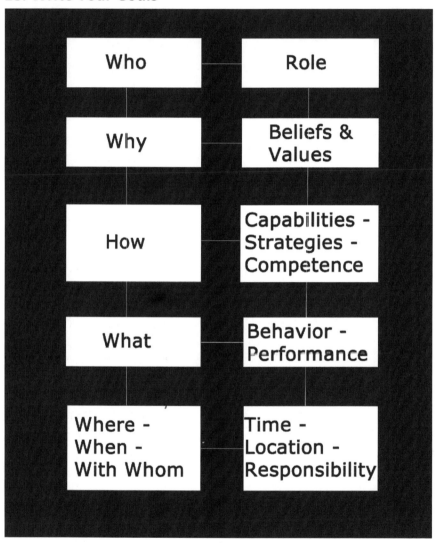

In chapters 21 through 26, we explored the five components to consider whenever setting a goal: Who, What, Why, How, and When, Where and With Whom. In this chapter we will finally use that information to set definitive goals.

Goal Cards

The goal card is a simple and incredibly powerful tool for writing and reaching your goals.

As you've learned, it's important to have goals . . . big and small, short-term and long-term, to enable you to achieve what you want. You've also learned that to effectively and quickly reach the goals that are of utmost importance to you, you must prioritize them on your list.

You need a way to stay centered on your most important goal(s), to get that goal burned into your subconscious mind. You can achieve this by having your goal(s) permanently available at arm's reach. A goal card is a great way to do that.

Using card stock, like an index card:
1. Write your deadline (the "When") at the top.
    For example: By August 15th of next year (or whenever your deadline is)
    (Note: This is the only part of your goal card that is written in future tense, and it's only for urgency. It's not part of your goal statement.)
    [The deadline you've created fosters a sense of urgency or purpose, which in turn will serve as an important motivator, and prevents inertia or procrastination]
2. Begin your goal statement by writing it in personal tense ("I")
3. Continue writing your goal in present tense ("I AM")
4. Write your goal with positive language and emotion ("I AM so happy")
5. Write your goal with gratitude ("I AM so happy and thankful")
6. Give added emphasis to personal and present tense ("I AM so happy and thankful now that I AM . . .")
7. Finish by filling in your goal, keeping the "Who," "Why", "How", "What," "Where", "When" and "With Whom" and your personal values list and mission and vision statements in mind.

Remember that the goal MUST be stated in the positive. In other words, you must write what you want to achieve, not what you want to avoid (how fit you want to become, not how much fat you want to get rid of).

Be as clear and specific as possible ("I will have supper with my family three nights a week" rather than, "I will be home earlier") and feel free to enrich and add as much emotion to your affirmation statement as possible. Ideally, when you read it, it should stir up a feeling and make a picture pop into your mind.

For instance, if your goal is to run a full marathon for the first time in your life, your goal statement might look like this:

My Goal:
By August 15th of next year,
I am so happy and thankful now that I am able to run a full marathon in Boston. My body is in great shape. I look radiant and very healthy, and I feel fantastic too. Everybody I speak with says they notice the positive change in me.
This might sound silly, but affirmations like these help to impress what you want upon your subconscious mind.

Assignment
For each of your most important goals, transfer it, in affirmation format, to a goal card.
If you have a laminator, you may wish to laminate your goal card for longevity purposes.
Keep your goal cards in front of you—affix them to your wall, desk or computer if you wish—to inspire you to take daily action.

—————————(Sidebar)—————————
Ensure the goal you work on is a key goal. Reaching it should contribute to your happiness in a major manner. Keep in mind that not all goals are created equal. Some are hardly important on the large scale of your happiness whilst others may highly contribute to it. A mere handful of your goals brings you a disproportionate large amount of happiness. Without goals, if you do achieve anything of value, it will be by chance, pure luck. Most of all, you can end up putting out a lot of time and effort for very little return.

Example: Goal Card

By September 15th 2013, I am so happy and excited to have finished my book on Goal Setting. It's finally available online!

Who
- Writing this book involves me in my role as Author

Why
- I want to publish this book as it fits perfectly with my mission statement to publish self-help books to help people live happy lives.
- I firmly believe people can change their lives for the better when they are informed. I value challenge and learning!

How
- the planning phase
- the outline phase
- preparing the first draft
- writing the first draft
- editing the first draft
- final review

Note: For each phase I'll plan individual short term goals

What:
I plan to write 1000 words a day, each working day.

Where, When & With Whom
- I will do research and writing in my home office
- I will make research, writing and editing my main focus in March, April and May 2013
- I will outsource editing

19. Long Term, Short Term Goals
Set goals with different time horizons

Every huge and life-changing goal requires distinctive smaller, mid and long-term goals. There are different ways of looking at the timeframes of these partial goals, but generally short-term goals should be understood as those things that can be achieved in a month. Mid-term goals should be possible to achieve within one year, and long-term goals are such things as earning a degree that usually take several years to accomplish. Furthermore, the different types of goals should also intertwine and build on each other.

Set your long-term goals first
By knowing your goals for the future, you will better understand your general direction in life and the big picture. These are the things that will take more patience and time to achieve. They will help you think ahead and imagine yourself in two, three, five or even twenty years. These are goals such as getting a job, saving up for university, graduating or finding a life partner.

When you know the general direction and the point where you want to get, you should set partial goals. Mid-term goals need to be broken down in terms of magnitude and time. If you, for instance, decide to lose 22 kg in a year, you may break it down to 11 kg in half a year and 5.5 kg in three months.

Short-term goals are less time-consuming and smaller. They usually take less than a year – several months, weeks, possibly even one day. The time frame of short-term goals is not precisely set, because these goals need to be evaluated in terms of context. If the long-term goal that encompasses the smaller goals is very lengthy, then these short-term goals are also going to be considerably time consuming. Smaller projects, however, break down into weekly or daily goals.

Some examples:

A long term goal could be: Be healthy, meaning having a BMI of 20 etcetera by January 2017
The short term goals could be: lose 20 lbs by January 2013 by walking 10.000 steps every day

A long term goal could be: Foster strong relationships
The short term goals could be: Spending 4 hours each week with my parents and other family starting in week 7 by entertaining at our house or visiting them in the weekends.

A long term goal could be: Have an enriching, fulfilling career in 5 years time.
The short term goals could be: get a job as a financial trader before January next year by finishing the requisite study and writing & sending 1 job request each week.

A long term goal could be: become more attractive.
The short term goals could be: losing 30lbs, 'buying more attractive clothes', 'improving my image', 'joining etiquette classes', 'improving my complexion"

20. Create An Action Plan

Goals you wrote and ordered in your journal are the beginnings of your **"action plan."**

Action plans are lists of responsibilities that instruct a person to carry out elements of short-term goals on a day-to-day basis; they will have a great deal to do with your day-to-day scheduling.

Action plans show the minute steps, the individual points between A and Z. They center your attention on the goals immediately needing achievement.

What does an action plan look like?
An action plan is simply a list of the most logical steps you need to take to achieve a short-term goal, in the order you need to take them.

—————————(Sidebar)—————————

Behavior is made up of the specific actions or reactions taken within our daily environment. Regardless of our capabilities, behavior describes what we actually do. It answers the question: what am I doing, what are my behaviors?

This has to do with the external context in which behavior occurs. It answers the question: when and where does this behavior occur? Where? When? With Whom? Where, when and with whom do you display your behaviors? What are the external influences on you?

Assignment

Write an action plan:
1. Choose one of your important long-term goals to work on. Read through each of its short-term goals, beginning with the first one you must carry out, and determine the minute steps you must take to accomplish that goal, in the order you must take them.

100

2. Write in list format the minute steps you must take, in the order you must take them. This list is your action plan for that goal.
3. If you find it motivates you, include a time frame for accomplishing each step. Be realistic so that you neither over- nor under-challenge yourself.
4. Begin with the first step of your action plan,
5. Check off each minute step you accomplish.
6. Do the same for all your medium and short-term goals, so that you may see the swiftness of your progress toward achieving your dream.

Congratulations! You have learned to focus your effort and energy in order to become a successful goal getter!

21. Why People Fail to Set and Achieve Goals

Despite inspiring dreams, despite energetic and motivating mission and vision statements, people can still fail to set and achieve goals. But what causes this to happen?
And what remedies will overcome it?

Here are the most common reasons people fail to set and achieve goals, and their remedies:

No perceived need.
Review Chapter Three, "Your Current State of Affairs." If you scored yourself 100 percent on all dimensions, there is no need for change. However, I have never met anyone who scored themselves 100 percent on all dimensions. So there must be room for improvement somewhere!

Not enough time.
When you are interested you do what is convenient. When you are committed you do whatever it takes.
Most people are only interested in dreaming of how life could be. They are not committed to doing whatever it takes to make those dreams a reality. Whether it is completing their planning, getting up early or staying late, they are just not committed. If you choose to simply go about your daily business—not making the time to set goals and fulfill them—then tomorrow will bring you exactly the same as it brought you today. If you do not make time for change, you are cheating yourself out of great opportunities.

Laziness.
In the short term, laziness can be considered an exaggeration of the natural instinct to get healthy rest, and conserve precious energy. It isn't something necessarily bad. But it is important to ask yourself if this state of mind and behavior will get you where you would like to be. Is the answer causing you pain or pleasure? Which do you prefer?

Illusion of busyness.
Too many interests and activities create an illusion of busyness but with no real focus or direction. Dare to be honest. What is this busyness bringing you in respect to happiness, joy, excitement, pleasure? If you have no real focus or direction, you will be moving but getting nowhere.

Wanting to please others.
Wanting to please others and always do what you think others want you to do rather than choosing to do what you want to do will hinder goal-setting and achievement. There may also be an imbalance in your relationships with others and in the outcome of these relationships. Quite often this wanting to please others will lead to a lose/win situation, with you on the losing end. You might be on your way to losing your own desires or even your own identity. My advice is, take another look at Chapter Three, "Your Current State of Affairs." You may be living an unbalanced life. Ask yourself how this makes you feel. If it does not feel good, it might be time for you to make a change. If you have difficulty breaking this habit and it is causing you trouble, please consider obtaining professional help.

Do not believe in your own ability to design and propel your own life.
If this is the case, you might be suffering from a lack of self-confidence. Just about everybody will suffer from a lack of self-confidence sometimes. Having a set of simple exercises you can practice during these times is an invaluable aid to getting your confidence level back on track as quickly as possible.

Here are six actions you can take to boost or maintain your confidence:

Don't give yourself a hard time. Don't be your own worst critic—be your own best friend. After all, if a friend of yours was going through a tough time, you would lift him up rather than tear him down. Positive self-talk can be one of your best tools for confidence-boosting, so make sure you cultivate the habit.

Remember a time when you felt confident. Confidence is a feeling, and if you've felt it once, you can feel it again. Remembering a time when you felt confident and in control will enable you to re-experience that feeling and help to put you in a confident frame of mind.

Practice. Whatever it is you want to feel confident about, practice it as often as you can. When you work on something until you could do it in your sleep, you can't fail to be confident in your ability to perform when it matters.

Practice correct posture. This might not sound like it's obviously related to confidence, but how you sit and how you stand sends a message out to those around you. If that message radiates confidence, you will get positive vibes back that will bolster your confidence. So learn to sit and stand like you have confidence.

Surround yourself with confident and positive people. It may seem self-evident, but if you are consistently mixing with people of low self-esteem, this is going to rub off on you. Conversely, if the people around you are upbeat and assured, this will create a positive atmosphere that you will benefit from.

Think about all the qualities you like about yourself and your talents and abilities. If you have any trouble doing this, think about the compliments you get from people: what do they say you do well? It's a good idea to write these positive characteristics down so you'll have them to refer to when your confidence is flagging and you need some inspiration. Make sure you give yourself due credit for these regularly—this will prove to be the best springboard for building unstoppable confidence.

Negative thinking.
Negative thinking includes any thoughts or forms of self-talk that include criticism, doubt, low expectations and put-downs. These thoughts usually stem from our insecurities and are repeated automatically by our subconscious mind many times throughout the day. If left unchallenged, these negative thoughts can lead to lack of

motivation, below average performance, self-doubt, and a tendency to fail.

If positive thinking can motivate you to succeed, it's possible that negative thinking can motivate you to fail. If we are capable of achieving anything that we believe, it stands to reason that if we believe we will fail, we can achieve that too.

So how do you beat negative thinking at its own game? The first step is to get to the source of the problem.

Negative thinking has two main origins: internal beliefs and external sources. The internal beliefs stem from any negative feelings that you may be harboring. The external sources can come from any person or event that caused you to become unsure of yourself or your abilities.

Most negative internal beliefs stem from insecurity. These insecurities can be based on events, honest mistakes or, more often, misconceptions. If these events are left unchallenged they can lead to feelings of low self-confidence, low self-esteem, and anxiety. Then, the next time that you experience a negative event, your insecurities use that event as fuel to reinforce the negative thoughts and feed your negative self talk.

So, how does internal negativity start? There are many causes, but they all share a general theme. Internal negativity stems from the way we react to any given situation.

Internal forces of negative thinking: Fear of what lies beyond your comfort zone.
Think back to when you were a child. Most of us have limitations put upon our lives in a very early stage. We are taught how to think, which schools to attend, how to make a living, and finally, even how to plan our retirement. Many of us end up fearing anything that is different from what we were taught.

For us to be able to change the things that we are unhappy with in our lives, we have to change the way that we think and act. If we never change the way that we think and act, we will continue to get the same results.

About ninety percent of people live their lives and never become the person that they dream of becoming. This happens simply because they fail to take action. They fear what they don't understand. We have to look at fear as nothing more than a word or a learning process. Mark Twain said it best with this quote: "Do the things that you fear most and the death to fear is certain." You owe it to yourself to overcome fear.

Begin with the small items that scare you. And gradually tackle the bigger issues. After doing so, you will look back and think how foolish it was to have been afraid in the first place.

Learn to leave your comfort zone. When we leave our comfort zone we become a more rounded individual. When we do the things we fear and look back at them afterward, we see—to our surprise—that what we feared has now turned into part of our comfort zone. The next time similar situations arise we will no longer stress over it, we will just do it.

We must set our minds to always conquer the unknown. Always think outside the box. Look fear in the eyes and just do the task. Every successful person has undoubtedly faced fear many times, yet they have succeeded in their endeavors. So can you.

Internal forces of negative thinking: Fear of not being good enough.
This source of negative thinking usually stems from our own misconceptions of how "good" others expect us to be. This misconception usually starts with a well-meaning parent or teacher who pushed you too hard when you were young. While they were most likely only trying to motivate you to always do your best, you may have been doing your best and came away from the experience feeling not good enough. It also comes from people who are judgmental or tear-you-downers. If we believe that others expect us to be perfect at all times, then even the most subtle failure could result in feelings of worthlessness, depression and anxiety.

The main problem with this insecurity is that our belief keeps us from realizing that it isn't others who are holding us to such high standards. This level of perfection is almost always self-imposed.

By harboring this misconception, you force yourself to perform in a constant state of overachievement. While the desire to overachieve can be great at times, it can also take away from your success. Why? Because perfection takes time. If you find yourself spending too much time on each and every decision or project, you could be robbing yourself of the chance to undertake or discover bigger and better opportunities. Also, perfectionists are unintentionally setting themselves up for a fall. No one can be perfect all the time. If you constantly hold yourself to this level of performance, you will eventually be disappointed. And, unfortunately, this disappointment can lead to an increase in negative thinking. So keep this in mind when you take action or plan goals. Often good is plenty good enough.

Internal forces of negative thinking: Fear of making a mistake.
The way we react to making a mistake can either strengthen our belief in our problem-solving skills or increase our negative views about ourselves. The difference comes from how we react to those mistakes. If you make a mistake, do you admit to it or do you run from it? Do you view it as a learning experience or as a reason to feel worthless? Do you see it as a just another experience or as an unavoidable happening based on your lack of skills?

If your prior experience with mistakes resulted in shame, then you will naturally harbor a fear of making mistakes. While you may use this fear as a way to protect yourself, it is a form of negative self-talk that can keep you from advancement and achievement. Think about that for a minute. If you are afraid to make a mistake, you will never try anything new, thus keeping yourself from discovering new opportunities and acting on great ideas.

Internal forces of negative thinking: Fear of failure.
But in some occasions, fulfillment of purpose is halted by fear, the fear that the purpose one is trying to fulfill won't be fulfilled due to personal failures. In other words, someone who feels that they have a

purpose that they must fulfill, might not attempt to do so because of fear due to lack of resources.

It is good to realize most successful people have failed miserably. That's right. At one time or another they have flopped, fell short, missed the mark, struck out or goofed up. Just "Google" for 'famous failures' and you'll notice I am not exaggerating. However, the difference between these people and the rest of the world is that when they failed, they made a choice to use the experience to better themselves. They determined to become stronger and to reach their goals.

Are you determined to reach your goal? Do you really believe you can achieve what you set out to accomplish? With determination and belief, you too can make the same choice to turn a failed situation into a winning one. How? By choosing to adapt a positive perspective and engage in edifying self-talk. Here are four phrases you can use to stay motivated when things don't go as you planned or wished them to:

1. "The only direction is up" or "It can't get any worse." Feel like you've hit rock bottom? Don't beat up on yourself too badly. To experience disappointment, heartbreak, embarrassment or self-doubt is to be human. However, to wallow in this state for too long is downright destructive. Tell yourself that it doesn't get much worse than this point, and let yourself know that the only place left to go is upward. Use failure as motivation to start climbing back up. When you do this, you will see that instead of running from failure, you will look it in the eye and overcome it.

"This is not the end of the line." Know this: everyone fails from time to time but failure is not the end of the line unless you allow it to be. You tried, you blundered, you failed and it hurts. Allow yourself time to grieve it, but then let it go so that you can get back to the business of reaching your intended goal. Remind yourself that the only positive option is to seek ways to turn the situation around. Then tell yourself that in the morning you will begin again!

"Hmmm, I may need to change direction." Does it seem like you've come to a roadblock? Then the solution may just be detouring and moving toward your goal in a different way. When something does not work out as planned, you may need to reevaluate the route you are taking. So review the situation, regroup, and get on a track around that roadblock. The track may be a different one, but it may also be a more successful one.

"I'll do better next time." As long as you're breathing, there's always room for improvement. Choose to use your failure as positive motivation to do better the next time around. When you remember your goal and envision reaching it, you will be super-charged to find ways to develop yourself. For example, if you need to do better in school, make (and follow) a consistent study schedule. If you are intent on a promotion at work, take classes to increase your skill set. No matter what the failed task consists of, you can use it to motivate yourself to get more done.

Internal forces of negative thinking: Fear of not being able to change.
A few lucky people do realize the reasons behind their negative thinking. However, they fail to recognize that these reasons can be changed. "I have never been any good at this kind of thing." "That's just the way I am." "I can't help how I think or feel." Do any of these statements sound familiar? These self-limiting statements stem from a fear of being unable to change. The statements afford us an excuse for our behavior. After all, if it can't be helped, then it can't be our fault.

The problem with these statements is that they limit us from achieving our true potential. If we believe the statements when we think them, then our reactions to them are almost always self-fulfilling. With these negative thoughts running through our minds, we are unable to accomplish certain goals even if we want to.

Internal forces of negative thinking: Fear of success.
Fear of success may sound like a strange idea, but many people can identify with the feelings below:
- Do you ever feel like something is holding you back?

- Do you find that you "get in your own way"?
- Do you feel real achievement is constantly just out of your grasp?

Now consider the positives and negatives you associate to being successful. For example, many people have the following associations to being successful:

- "If I became financially successful I might not be spiritual."
- "If I became successful I might lose my family."
- "If I became successful I might have a lot more pressure on me to perform, as well as a lot more pressure on my time, and I might not have time to do what I want to do."

This fear of success can result in:

- Losing the motivation or the desire to grow, achieve, and succeed
- A lack of effort to achieve goals you have set for yourself in school, on the job, at home, in relationships, or in your personal growth
- Problems making decisions, being unable to solve problems
- Chronic underachievement
- Self-destructive behavior: tripping yourself up to make sure you do not keep a certain level of success or achievement you once had in school, on the job, at home, in relationships, or in your personal growth
- Feeling guilt, confusion, and anxiety when you do achieve success. This leads you to falter, waver, and eventually lose your momentum

Fear of success is all about conflicting beliefs. In the event of conflicting beliefs, the stronger ones will always override the weaker ones.

Your dominant beliefs have the true authority over your reality creation.

We know that conflicting beliefs can be a source of self-sabotage. But conflicting beliefs may only slow you down and not entirely stop you from achieving success. Whether self-sabotage kills you or not depends on the collective strength of your empowering beliefs against that of your disempowering ones.

The more harmonious beliefs you have and the less conflicting ones, the faster you will be able to achieve success in the area that those beliefs have relevance to.

External forces of negative thinking.
Now that we have identified the internal sources of negative thinking, let's examine the external sources. These sources can be easier to recognize but a little harder to control. Nevertheless it's good to know what you may run into as you begin your goal-setting career.

External sources of negative thinking come from outside ourselves but their true harm comes from the way we react to these sources.

Think about this for a minute. We cannot always control what happens to us, or the people we meet, but we can control how we react to each of these events.
For example, if you are thinking about introducing a new product to your business but everyone you share the idea with has a negative opinion about it, your reaction may be to second-guess your idea. Or, if you are about to undertake a new exercise program, but your spouse comments that you will never stick with it, your subconscious may believe him or her and your reaction may be to lose your motivation.

While those examples show how another person's comments can induce negative thinking, events can also have the same effect. Say, for example, that you did introduce a new product but it didn't sell well. The event could play on your insecurities and your reaction might be to think negatively about yourself and your business abilities.

Or, if you started an exercise program but didn't see the results that you wanted, your reaction might be to fall into a trap of thinking it was your fault. Your insecurities could cause you to think, "I knew I couldn't do it" or "Nothing I ever do turns out right."

Events that are even farther beyond your control can also be a source of negative thinking. For instance, if you were laid off from your job because of downsizing, negative thoughts can begin to form from that event. Although the layoff had nothing to do with you or your abilities personally, the event can still lead you to form a negative opinion about yourself. One scenario would be to decide that you were cursed with bad luck. If you were to continue believing this, then you might shy away from new opportunities or automatically talk yourself into failing at your next job.

As you can see, each of these sources or insecurities can lead to negative thinking. The key is to learn to recognize these insecurities. Recognizing insecurities and knowing that they are very common makes it easier to cope with them before they stop you from achieving what you want.

Obstacles to "Why."
Just as you considered the most important benefits you will receive by reaching your goal you also need to consider the most important obstacles you could encounter in your journey toward goal completion.

It's not a question of whether you will have roadblocks; it's a question of what and when, and whether or not you will prevail. That's why your "Why" must be strong—to take you through those challenges so you can reach your goals.

Obstacles, as we just learned, can be internal (coming from your limiting beliefs, doubts or fears) or external (caused by events or people). Here's how to make the distinction. Ask yourself:
- "What past conditioning and old beliefs are standing in my way?"
- "What am I saying to me that is standing in my way?"

If appropriate, you might benefit from consulting with a certified practitioner who specializes in helping people to clear old limiting beliefs, hurtful past events, and negative conditioning.

If you believe you are not successful in achieving a goal list every obstacle you can think of that could stop you from achieving each goal. For example: no time to cook better food, too heavy of a schedule, drop-in visitors, procrastination, improper scheduling, lack of discipline, unexpected work requirements, friends expect me to drink with them, bad eating habits.

Now list insights you discovered in this chapter that might help you to get around, or to overcome, those obstacles.

22. Commit To Life's Goals

To commit to your life's goals, make the following agreements with yourself:

- You are serious about setting and reaching your goals.
- You promise yourself that you will consistently use the skills learned to help you set and reach the wonderful success you deserve.
- You agree to be honest with yourself and positive in your outlook.
- You will be true to your values and design your goals around your roles.
- You will set a new goal whenever one is reached.
- You will not blame your upbringing, education, other people or circumstances when goal setting becomes difficult.
- If necessary, you will seek out a coach or mentor to assist if you really get stuck.
- You will do your best to maintain a positive and optimistic outlook, even in the face of negative events.
- You are willing to gain and maintain the habit of using the simple learned skills to reach your goals of happiness and fulfillment.
- You recognize that to reach your goals, you must grow personally, so you commit to consistently seek to increase your knowledge by reading, listening, and watching motivational and educational material and to taking courses which will give you a positive attitude and a leading edge in learning and applying that knowledge to increase your personal power and the results you get.
- You will keep a list of all these activities and evaluate their usefulness regularly.
- You are truly excited about the difference this will make as you direct, organize and manage your life toward success.

A few people have remarked that the method used in this book seems like a lot of hassle. And, yes, it does take a little thought and care to create a goal that is clear and achievable.

But if your goal isn't worth this amount of thought is it worthwhile going after in the first place?

Doing it this way takes a bit longer and requires more preparation, but it makes reaching your goal a lot easier since the process will focus your mind and will motivate you to achieve it.

Having a clear and carefully defined goal significantly increases the odds that you will achieve your goal. This way or defining your outcome changes it from being a pipe dream to being a target.

23. Character Matters

No worldly possessions can make up for a lack of character.
Character implies integrity and integrity means you do right- even
when there is no one is paying attention.

This means you live by the rule "do to others as you would like them
do to you". This rule should be part of your life.

Give it some thought.
Have you ever been lured to shortcut your way to achieve
something? Reaching that goal is a marvelous achievement, but if
you stepped on to many people on the way up be prepared to be
stepped on in return one day.

Do you normally treat people with respect and honesty? Or do you
have a short fuse when you have to deal with those who won't bow
to your every wish and command?

Anyone with integrity and character will never have to be worried
about this since they realize that no one achieves good results
without the help of others.

Whether it's success in business, in sports or in raising a family,
someone was probably there to offer a assistance along the way. A
person with character and integrity will know and appreciate this and
offer the same helping hand when the opportunity arises.

What does success mean to you?

Character is what you are. Success is what you achieve. Success
attained without showing character and integrity is an empty shell.
Your character matters as you work toward your goals, and it is a
quality that will inspire those who surround you. So let your strength
of character shine through in your walk and talk and you will be
able to achieve great successes.

24. Goal Setting: Final Insights

We began this book with the dreams we wanted to set goals to achieve and the aspects of ourselves we wanted to set goals to improve. Then we wrote mission and vision statements, then solidified and wrote our goals, taking into consideration "Who," "What," "Why," "How," ,"Where","When" and "With Whom". We used this process to explain the goal setting process from an educational point of view, keeping the steps simple and clear.

Outside the classroom we sometimes work differently. The human brain doesn't always use a chronological or hierarchic approach. It often uses a more indefinable approach. This means it might come up with a goal statement first before even considering the obstacles or the role. The next time it might use an unsatisfied role and search for a goal and benefits to satisfy it. In other words, every goal might originate from a different place. Feel free to let them. Just remember it is important that you give all elements consideration when you choose a new goal.

Our education system focuses on filling our heads with data, facts, and figures. The learner is often passive. Goal setting requires assessment and problem solving skills. Goal setting involves application and organization. The learner is active and requires original thinking, lateral thoughts, personal independence, and responsibility.
Goal setting is a formal process for personal planning. By setting goals on a routine basis you will decide what you want to achieve, and then, step by step, you will move toward achieving those goals.

Goals are what will keep you motivated and focused—both essential to being productive. Think of goals and aims as necessary achievements. In achieving your desired goals, you should start with a positive outlook. You must be excited with the challenges and tasks that you have to do to give you the right start or motivation. As you proceed on the roadmap to success and happiness, just be sure to keep your goals realistic; do not try to do everything at once. You can't drive to two different cities at once; neither should you try to accomplish too many goals at once or you will find yourself feeling pulled apart and overwhelmed.

How many long-term goals should you be working on? Two or three, maximum. If you attempt more it will become increasingly difficult to make time for good quality actions to achieve those goals.

For each new, future goal, I recommend you work through the goal setting process outlined in this book, until you have worked through the process a few times and are comfortable with it. This will take some time and will force you to fully concentrate on all the elements of successful goal setting. It's like Confucius said, "I see, I forget. I hear, I remember. I do, I understand." You have to do it to understand how it works and to master it. Once you have mastered it you will be able to enjoy it and reap the benefits.

As you get more experienced you might be able to skip some steps. Especially when your goals have common denominators. After all, you can always work through the entire process when you are thinking of planning a goal in a territory you are not familiar with.

Hold on to a journal.
On days when the going gets tough, and your enthusiasm for goal setting wears thin, your journal will be there to remind you what it's all about. Your mission and vision statements are there, as are your dreams. You have recorded them, to enable you to move forward, and so you can read them on a rainy day.
You can follow your progress and gain courage from it.
If you commit to your written goals and are diligent, you are half way to accomplishing happiness and success.

In Conclusion
People who set goals and follow up on them are usually better capable living their life to the fullest.

Just think of time you set a goal and steadily worked toward it to ultimate success: the thrill of losing weight, completing a marathon, planning a great wedding to look back on, starting a home-based business, saving money or earning a college degree, and feeling fulfilled and happy with your achievements.

How many of the following applied to you then:
- Steadily moving toward and achieving the results you want by losing a pound each week
- Clear and focused direction giving you a sense of accomplishment and purpose when you trained for the marathon
- High enthusiasm for what you had in mind as you planned your wedding
- Boosted self-esteem, confidence and belief in your ability to make it happen and feeling in control by finally saving money instead of getting into debt
- Efficient and effective use of your time preparing for your exam

These are just a few of the many benefits you will reap from your newfound knowledge of goal-setting.

Keep in mind:
60% of people do not set goals.
10% of people set goals, but do not write them down.
3% of people set goals and write them down and act . . .
and the 3% does 50 times better than all the others put together!
Welcome to the 3% Club.

25. Goal Setting and Time Management

Goal setting and time management are two different concepts, but they are practically inter-related and inter-twined.

Time management would not be effective and achievable without goal setting.

Goal setting, for its part, needs effective time management skills for it to be successfully achieved.

Remember, when managing your time, the first thing you should attend to would be assessing or setting out your list of priorities. Doing so would enable you to carry out tasks that need to be carried out first than the others.

It is impossible for anyone to set priorities without first setting goals. Priorities are things that should be given primary and foremost focus and attention. The same goes for goals.

There are several good books available on the topic of TimeManagement. If you enjoyed this book on Goal Setting you might want to check out Raymond Le Blanc's book on Time Management.

How to Get in Contact

Well, you have reached the end of this book, but not the end of your learning. Please share with me your successes. I'd love to hear about them. I hope you enjoyed reading this book as much as I enjoyed creating it. You are already ahead of most people because you care enough to learn more. Now all you have to do is go out and use this knowledge. I would like to see you have tremendous success!

You can reach me by using the contact information you will find http://raymond-le-blanc.com

http://twitter.com/raymondleblanc

Special Note from the Author

My Personal Thank You!

I thank you for purchasing "Goal Setting Success Secrets" and would love to hear from you. If you enjoyed the information in this book, it would be much appreciated to hear what you think. So I encourage you to leave a quick review to let others know what you liked in this book.

Thank you for your help and time and look out for the other book in this series called: "Time Management Tips, Tools & Techniques."

Bibliography

Books

Allen, David. Getting Things Done. New York: Penguin Books, 2001.

Babauta, Leo. The Power of Less. New York. Hyperion. 2009

Bradbury, Andrew. Develop your NLP Skills. London. Kogan. 2006

Bruce, Andy & Langdon, Ken. Simplify Your Life. New York. DK Publishing. 2001

Bruno, Dave. The 100 Thing Challenge. New York. HarperCollins. 2010

Canfield, Jack and Janet Switzer. How to Get From Where You Are to Where You Want to Be. New York: HarperCollins Publishers, 2007.

Covey, S. R., Merrill, A. R. & Merrill, R. R. (1994). "First Things First." New York: Fireside.

Covey, Stephen R. The Seven Habits of Highly Effective People: Restoring the Character Ethic. New York: Simon & Schuster, 1989.

Davenport, Liz. Order from Chaos: A Six-Step Plan for Organizing Yourself, Your Office, and Your Life. New York. Three Rivers Press, 2001.

Dilts, Robert. Verander Je Overtuigingen. Andromeda, 2006.

Dodd, Pamela and Doug Sundheim. The 25 Best Time Management Tools & Techniques: How to Get More Done Without Driving Yourself Crazy. Ann Arbor, MI: Peak Performance Press, Inc., 2005.

Ferriss, Timothy. The 4-Hour Workweek: Escape 9-5, Live Anywhere, and Join the New Rich. New York: Crown, 2007.

Forsyt, Patrick. 100 Great Time Management Ideas. Singapore. Marshall Cavendish. 2009

Grenier, Marc. GoalPro Success Guide. Initial Publishing, 2000.

Guillebeau, Chris. The Art of Non-Conformity. London. Perigee. 2011

Harris, Carol. NLP An Introductory Guide to the Art and Science of Excellence. Element Books, 2000.

Haynes, Marion E. Persoonlijk Tijdmanagement. Academic Service, 2000.

Hindle, Tim. Manage Your Time. New York. DK Publishing 1998

Joyner, Mark. Simpleology. The Simple Science of getting What you Want. New Jersey. John Wiley & Sons, 2007

Kelsey, Robert. What's Stopping You, Chichester. Capstone Publishing. 2011

Kievit-Broeze, Ineke E. Effectief Tijdbeheer. Handleiding voor praktisch time- en self-management. Schoonhoven: Academic Service, 1998.

Kustenmacher, Werner Tiki. Simplify Your Life. Munchen. Knauer. 2008

Linden, Anné and Kathrin Perutz. Mindworks: NLP Tools for Building a Better Life. Kansas City, MO: Andrews McMeel,1997.

Mancini, Marc. Time Management. Madison, WI: CWL Publishing Enterprises, Inc., 2003.

Millman, Dan. The Life You Were Born to Live: A Guide to Finding Your Life Purpose. H J Kramer,1993.

Pollar, Odette. Organizing Your Work Space, Revised Edition: A Guide to Personal Productivity. Mississauga, Ontario, Canada: Crisp Learning, 1998.

Seerup, Kevin, et al. GoalMaker. The Complete Goal Management System, Experience the Possibilities. Access Able Systems,1997.

Seiwert, Lothar J. Het 1+1 van Tijd-Management. Time/system,1988.

Seiwert, Lothar, Time-Management. Aartselaar. ZuidNederlandse Uitgevery 2002

Smith, Hyrum W. What Matters Most: The Power of Living Your Values. New York: Simon & Schuster, 2001.

Turkington, Carol A. Stress management for Busy People. McGraw-Hill,1998.

Vaklin, Shlomo, The Big Book of NLP, Inner Patch Publishing,2010

Web Pages

How the World's Richest 1% Get More Done by Working Less - And Less Hard, Too., http://www.simpleology.com/indexs16.php (2007-04-11)

Interactive Wheel of Life.
http://www.jamuna.com/InteractiveWheel.swf (2007-04- 13)
"Law of Attraction." Wikipedia,
http://en.wikipedia.org/wiki/Law_of_Attraction (2007-04-11)
Living Congruently,
http://www.stevepavlina.com/blog/2005/02/living-congruently/
(2012-08-01)
NLP Meta Programs,
http://www.nlpls.com/articles/metaPrograms.php (2012-08-01)
Personal "Energy Audit." http://ozpk.tripod.com/0000emotion
(2007-04-11)
Seven NLP Meta-Programs for Understanding People,
http://sourcesofinsight.com/seven-meta-programs-for-understanding-
people/ (2012-08-01)
Simpleology 101 Review.
http://www.soulselfhelp.com/simpleology-101.html (2007- 04-11)
Success Discoveries. http://www.successdiscoveries.com/ (2008-09-
24)
The Science of Goal Achievement.
http://www.ironmagazine.com/article177.html
Walker, Karen. http://www.karenwalkercoaching.com (2007-04-11)
Wheel of Life. http://www.rainbow-journey.org/cgi-
bin/multiradar.pl (2007-04-11)
Worksheets to Help You Create Your Own Internet Lifestyle Plan,
http://www.mymarketingcoach.com/goalworksheets.pdf (accessed
November 19, 2011)

Audio
Allen, David. Ready for Anything: 52 Productivity Principles for
Work and Life (Audio CD), Simon & Schuster Audio,2003.
Bliss, Edward C. Doing It Now (4 Pack) Cassette: How To Cure
Procrastination And Achieve Your Goals In Twelve Easy Steps,
Simon & Schuster Audio, 1987.
Morgenstern, Julie. Time Management from the Inside Out,
Abridged edition, Simon & Schuster Audio, 2000.
How to Manage Priorities and Meet Deadlines (Audio Seminars)
(Audio Cassette). Nightingale Conant, 1993.

Other Books by Raymond Le Blanc

http://www.amazon.com/Raymond-Le-Blanc/e/B002BT9FS6/

About The Author

Raymond Le Blanc holds a master's degree in economics from the Erasmus University Rotterdam and a master's degree in clinical psychology from the Open University in Heerlen. He is also a NLP master practitioner.

He was born and raised in Kuala Lumpur, Malaysia before his family left for Europe.

Raymond is an international author who publishes books on a broad range of topics. Mostly self-help or self-improvement related.

Book titles include "Autism & Asperger's Syndrome in Layman's Terms", "Understanding and Overcoming Anxiety and Panic Attacks", "Singapore. The Socio-Economic Development Of A City-State: 1960-1980" and "Depressief? Heb je last van een dipje of is het depressiviteit? (Dutch)".

After pursuing a career in banking, Raymond switched emphasis to combine his passions. He now coaches people to develop and lead fulfilling lives and writes (non)fiction.

Raymond lives with his wife Karin and their two children, Brigitte and Vincent, in a rural area of The Netherlands.

Made in the USA
Lexington, KY
04 January 2013